OXFORD
LATIN
COURSE

PART I
SECOND EDITION

MAURICE BALME & JAMES MORWOOD

OXFORD
UNIVERSITY PRESS

OXFORD
UNIVERSITY PRESS

Great Clarendon Street, Oxford OX2 6DP

Oxford University Press is a department of the University of Oxford.
It furthers the University's objective of excellence in research, scholarship,
and education by publishing worldwide in

Oxford New York
Auckland Bangkok Buenos Aires Cape Town Chennai
Dar es Salaam Delhi Hong Kong Istanbul Karachi Kolkata
Kuala Lumpur Madrid Melbourne Mexico City Mumbai Nairobi
São Paulo Shanghai Singapore Taipei Tokyo Toronto

with an associated company in Berlin

Oxford is a registered trade mark of Oxford University Press
in the UK and in certain other countries

© Oxford University Press 1996
Reprinted 1997 (twice), 1999, 2000, 2001, 2002

ISBN 0 19 912226 1

Typeset and designed by Positif Press, Oxford
Printed in Italy

Contents

Acknowledgements

The publisher and authors would like to thank the many consultants
in the United Kingdom and the United States for comments and
suggestions that have contributed towards this second edition.
In particular: (UK) Julian Morgan, Deborah Bennett, David Cartwright,
Alison Doubleday, John Powell, Philip Powell, Jeremy Rider, Tim
Reader, F. R. Thorn, Andrew Wilson; (US) John Gruber-Miller, Carlos
Fandal, Dennis Herer, James Lowe, Diana Stone and Jeffrey Wills.

*The publishers would like to thank the following for permission to
reproduce photographs*:

British Museum p.1, p.23, p.39; Musée Calvet, Avignon p.10; Tony Souter/
Hutchison Library p.11; H L Pierce Fund, courtesy, Museum of Fine Arts,
Boston p.12; Scala, Florence p.14, p.26 (*left*), p.33, p.35, p.46, p.59, p.79, p.90,
p.99; The Metropolitan Museum of Art, Fletcher Fund, 1931, (31.11.10)
(Photograph by Schecter Lee) ©1986, Metropolitan Museum of Art p.15; Villa
dei Misteri, Pompeii/The Bridgeman Art Library, London p.17; British
Museum/The Bridgeman Art Library, London p.19; Hulton Deutsch Collection
p.26 (*right*); Roger Dalladay p.27, p.28 (*top and centre*), p.85 (*bottom*), p.98,
p.103; Bildarchiv Preussischer Kulturbesitz p.28 (*bottom*) p.66 (*bottom*), p.95;
Foto Mairani/Grazia Neri p.29; Spectrum Colour Library p.32, p.45; Alfredo
Dagli Orti/Bildarchiv Preussischer Kulturbesitz p.34; Musee d'Archéologie,
Algeria/G Dagli Orti p.36; Rheinisches Landesmuseum, Trier p.38; Musée du
Louvre/Bonora-Giraudon pp.40–41, p.65, p.85 (*top*); James Morwood p.47,
p.65, p.84 (*bottom right*); Peter Clayton p.50, p.55, p.58, p.84 (*bottom left*),
p.86; Eric Dugdale p.51; Kunsthistorisches Museum, Vienna p.53; AKG/Erich
Lessing, Mykonos, Museum p.56; M Pucciarelli, Rome p.57, p.83; GeoScience
Features Picture Library p.62; Gift in Honour of Edward W Forbes from His
Friends. Courtesy, Museum of Fine Arts, Boston p.63; Michael Holford p.66
(*top*); Edinburgh University Library p.68; Biblioteca Ambrosiana, Milan p.70;
Biblioteca Apostolica Vaticana (Ms Lat 3225 fol. XIIIr) p.72; Musée du
Louvre/Giraudon p.76; The Somerset County Museum, Taunton Castle p.77;
John Brennan, Oxford p.78; Ancient Art and Architecture Collection p.82;
AKG/Erich Lessing. Athens, National Archaeological Museum p.84 (*top*);
Alinari-Giraudon p.88; Musée du Louvre/Lauros-Giraudon pp.92–93;
Fitzwilliam Museum, Cambridge p.106.

Cover photo: Scala

The cartoons are by Cathy Balme.
The illustrations are by Peter Connolly (pp. 48 and 57)
and Richard Hook (pp. 21, 32, 73, 89, 97 and 105).
The maps were drawn by John Brennan.

Introduction

This course tells the story of the life of the Roman poet known to us as Horace. His full name was Quintus Horatius Flaccus, but in this course we call him simply Quintus. Part I tells the story of his childhood and early schooling in his home-town, Venusia, in south-east Italy. In Part II his father takes him to Rome for his secondary education; after this he goes to university in Athens, but when civil war breaks out he leaves university to join the army. In Part III, when his side in the war is defeated, he returns to Italy, begins to write poetry, and eventually becomes one of the leading poets of his time and a friend of the emperor Augustus. You will learn more about his life in the first background essay (pp. 11–12).

We have chosen the life of Horace as the subject of this book both because he was an interesting person who tells us a lot about himself in his poetry, and because he lived through one of the most exciting periods of Roman history; in his time he saw the assassination of Julius Caesar, the destruction of the old republic and the establishment of the empire.

The story is told in Latin, the language of the Romans; it was spoken throughout the Roman empire, which stretched from Syria in the east to Britain in the north. Latin is one of a large family of languages to which English and nearly all European languages belong, as well as Indian and Persian. Anglo-Saxon, from which English is directly descended, is only distantly related to Latin and is not much like it. But about one half of the words in modern English are not Anglo-Saxon in origin, but borrowed from Latin at various stages of our history. Some of these words can hardly be fully understood unless you know some Latin; a knowledge of Latin will help you to spell and understand English better. Equally, when you are reading Latin, the meaning of many Latin words from which English words are derived is immediately obvious; for instance, (Latin) **parēns** = (English) parent; (Latin) **accūsō** = (English) I accuse.

One good reason, then, for learning Latin is that a knowledge of Latin will improve your understanding of English. It is also a help in learning foreign languages, since Italian, Spanish and French are directly descended from Latin and have many features in common with it. Above all, the history and literature of the Romans are interesting in themselves and still important to us. Our civilization is descended from theirs, and we can see their influence at many points both in our literature and in our lives today. You may be surprised to find that, in spite of the great differences between their way of life and ours, there are many similarities; we probably have more in common with a Roman of

Horace's day than with an Englishman of the Middle Ages. Lastly, to read and understand Latin, you need to think clearly; this is a skill which is essential in all academic subjects and, indeed, in the whole of life. It would be wrong to pretend that Latin is easy but we hope that our course will make the process of learning it both interesting and enjoyable.

In learning any foreign language it is essential to pronounce the language correctly. Latin sounded very much like modern Italian or Spanish. Most of the consonants were pronounced much as they are in modern English, but the vowel sounds were like those of Italian.

Consonants

c is always hard, as in **c**at (never soft as in ni**c**e).

g is always hard, as in **G**od (except when it is followed by **n**; **gn** is sounded **ngn**, as in ha**ngn**ail, so **magnus** is pronounced **mangnus**).

h is always sounded, as in **h**ope.

i is used as a consonant as well as a vowel; as a consonant it sounds like English **y**; so Latin **iam** is pronounced **yam**.

q is never found except when followed by **u**, sounded as in English **qu**ick.

r is rolled, as in Scottish, and is always sounded, so in Latin **sors**, for example, both **r** and **s** are sounded.

s is always soft, as in **s**it (never like **z**, as in ro**s**e).

v is pronounced like English **w**; so **vidi** sounds **weedee**.

The other consonants are pronounced like their English equivalents.

Where double consonants occur, as in si**tt**ing, both consonants are pronounced; so i**ll**e is pronounced **il-le** (**l** is sounded twice).

Vowels

The five vowels each have a long and a short version:

a short, as in English c**u**p (not as in c**a**p).

ā long, as in English f**a**ther.

e short, as in English p**e**t.

ē long, as in English **ai**m (French g**ai**).

i short, as in English d**i**p.

ī long, as in English d**ee**p.

o   short, as in English p**o**t.

ō   long, as in English f**oa**l (French b**eau**).

u   short, as in English p**u**t.

ū   long, as in English f**oo**l.

To make pronunciation easier, we have throughout the course put a long mark (ā, ē, ī, ō, ū) over all long vowels; all vowels without such a mark are short.

Now sound aloud the five vowels in Latin pronunciation, each one first in short form, then in long. Do this several times until you are thoroughly familiar with the sounds.

The vowel sounds in Latin are constant, that is to say short **a** is always pronounced as in c**u**p, long **ā** always as in f**a**ther, etc.

Next say aloud the following Latin words with correct vowel sounds:

amat, amāmus, bibō, cēna, colō, comes, ducis, dūcō, ferimus, fīlia, pācis, pōnō, prīmus, lūce, lītus.

Read again what is said above about consonants and say aloud the following Latin words:

vēnī, vīdī, vīcī, vīnum, rēgis, partem, urbis, morte, patres, carmen, iam, iaciō, eius, cuius, magnus, possum, annus, mittō, immemor, succurrō, immortālis.

Diphthongs

A diphthong is two vowels making one sound:

ae   as in English h**igh**.

au   as in English h**ow**.

ei   as in English **ei**ght.

eu   e-u (not a proper diphthong – both vowels are sounded).

oe   as in English b**oy**.

ui   u-i (both vowels are sounded).

Read aloud the following Latin words:

altae, puellae, laudat, caelum, nautae, heu, foedus, deinde, huic, pauper, saepe.

Read aloud the first story in the course (p. 10: *Scintilla and Horatia at home*); do this several times, until you are fluent in pronunciation. At first read slowly and then at an ordinary English reading speed. Always **READ ALOUD** all the Latin you meet before attempting to translate it. Latin should sound like a foreign language (most like Italian), not a debased kind of English.

8

Scintilla and Horatia at home

Vītam nārrāmus Quīntī Horātī Flaccī. lēctor, attende et fābulā gaudē.
(We are telling the story of the life of Quintus Horatius Flaccus.
Reader, pay attention and enjoy the story.)

What English words come from **nārrāmus**, **attende**, **fābulā**?

Quīntus est puer Rōmānus.

Quīntus in Apūliā habitat; Apūlia est in Italiā.

Scintilla est fēmina Rōmāna; in casā labōrat.

Horātia puella Rōmāna est; in casā cēnat.

A very large number of English words are derived from Latin. Your knowledge of English will often enable you to see immediately the meaning of unknown Latin words and your knowledge of Latin will often enable you to recognize the meaning of difficult English words.

For instance, from Latin **habitat** are derived English 'habitation', 'inhabit' etc., so that you can see immediately that the Latin word must mean 'lives', 'dwells'; from **labōrat** come English 'labour' etc., so that the Latin word must mean 'works'. What is (a) a *laborious* task (b) *puerile* behaviour (c) *feminine* intuition? From which Latin word is each of the English words in italics derived? What do the Latin words mean?

Vocabulary 1 *Learn the following words*

verbs		*adjectives*	
ambulat	he/she walks	**fessa**	tired
cēnat	he/she dines	**laeta**	happy
festīnat	he/she hurries	**parāta**	ready
intrat	he/she enters		
labōrat	he/she works	*adverbs*	
		mox	soon
nouns		**nōn**	not
casa	house, cottage		
cēna	dinner	*conjunctions*	
fēmina	woman	**et**	and
puella	girl	**sed**	but

A family meal

Scintilla and Horatia at home

Read aloud, understand and translate the following passage

Scintilla in casā labōrat; fessa est. Horātia in casam intrat; iēiūna est. sed cēna nōn parāta est. Scintilla festīnat et mox cēna est parāta.

'ecce!' inquit, 'cēna est parāta.' puella laeta est; ad mēnsam festīnat et avidē cēnat.

postrīdiē Scintilla ad tabernās ambulat. Horātia in casā labōrat. mox Scintilla redit et in casam intrat. ecce, parāta est cēna. Scintilla laeta est.

in casam	into the house
iēiūna	hungry
ecce!	look!; **inquit** she says
ad mēnsam	to the table
avidē	greedily
postrīdiē	the next day
ad tabernās	to the shops
redit	returns

5

QUINTUS

Quintus, the hero of our story, actually existed. His full name was Quintus Horatius Flaccus and in English he is usually called Horace. He was born on 8 December 65 BC in Venusia, a large town in the wild area of Apulia in south-east Italy. His father, whom he loved and admired, was a freedman, somebody who had been a slave and then been given his freedom; he was an auctioneer's agent who owned a small farm. But we know nothing at all about any other relatives. We have invented the name Scintilla for Quintus' mother and given him a sister called Horatia.

Apulia

In telling the story of Quintus we have made up many details. But much of our story is true. We know from his own poetry that his father did not send him to the local school – though in our story we pretend that he did go there for a while – but 'he dared to take me to Rome as a boy to be taught the arts which any father from the top levels of society would have his own sons taught'. In Rome Flaccus took him to what was perhaps the best school, that of Orbilius. After this he may have studied rhetoric, the art of public speaking, which was the usual form of tertiary education. Finally, when he was about twenty, his father sent him to the Academy in Athens, the most famous university of the ancient world, where he studied philosophy. No wonder Horace always speaks of him with gratitude and affection.

At the age of twenty-one he ended his career as a student in Athens and joined the army of Marcus Brutus, the leading assassin of Julius Caesar. Thus when he was twenty-two he fought as a military tribune – a surprisingly high rank – and even commanded a legion on the losing side in one of the bloodiest battles of the ancient world, at Philippi in north-east Greece (42 BC).

After this humiliation, he returned to Rome, became a clerk in the Treasury and started to write poetry. This led him to move in literary circles where he met Virgil, the greatest of the Roman poets. Virgil introduced him to Maecenas, one of the most powerful men of the time and a great patron of the arts. Maecenas became a close friend and presented him with a farm in the Sabine hills near Rome, and his support allowed Horace to devote himself entirely to writing poetry.

Through Maecenas, he became a friend of Augustus, the first Roman emperor, who admired his poetry and even asked him to become his private secretary. Horace refused the position, but remained on good terms with Augustus. So the son of a humble freedman from a remote part of Italy rose to become the friend of the greatest men in Rome. He owed this extraordinary success partly to his character. Maecenas undoubtedly had a deep affection for him, but it was his poetry which brought him to Maecenas' notice and his poetry which made him an influence in the Rome of Augustus.

Horace did not write a vast number of poems; in fact they fit into one slim volume. But they are highly original – they include four books of Odes, which he modelled on Greek lyric poetry, two books of Satires, in which he laughs either at himself or at the follies of his fellow men, and two books of Epistles, letters to friends in poetic form. At the end of the first set of Odes which he published, he proudly claims:

> I have raised a monument more lasting than bronze and higher than the ruins of the royal pyramids. Neither biting rain nor the wild north wind nor the innumerable procession of the years can destroy it … Not all of me shall die … a man who became powerful from humble beginnings …

In his poetry he tells us a good deal about himself as a man. He was, he says, short, fat and quick-tempered; the one surviving portrait of him suggests that he was not as unattractive as he claims. He had a wide circle of friends who were devoted to him and, although he never married, he had many love affairs. He is always apt to laugh at himself; for instance, he ends one epistle to a friend: 'When you want a laugh, you can visit me, fat and sleek, a pig from Epicurus' sty.' Epicurus was the philosopher who said that pleasure was the purpose of life, and Horace sometimes claimed to follow this philosophy. But Epicurus' philosophy wasn't just about enjoying life: it recommended moderation in all things. In fact it was the simple pleasures of country life that most appealed to Horace, who was happier working on his Sabine farm than living it up in Rome. He died not long after Maecenas on 27 November 8 BC at the age of fifty-six.

Quintus Horatius Flaccus

What he was like as a child we can only guess, and in the first part of this course the story is fictional; but in the second part it gradually draws closer to historical fact and we hope that by the end, partly through quotations from his own poetry, a true picture of his character emerges.

Horace's outlook on life can be summed up in his own words 'carpe diem, quam minimum crēdula posterō' *(seize every day, giving no thought for tomorrow). What do you think about his approach to living?*

Scintilla in casā labōrat; cēnam parat.

Horātia casam intrat; Scintillam salūtat.

Horātia Scintillam iuvat; aquam in casam portat.

Argus casam intrat et Horātiam salūtat.

Notice the change in word endings, e.g. **Horāti-a**, **Scintill-am**. Why do the endings change?
Compare English: '<u>We</u> help them.' 'They help <u>us</u>.'

Vocabulary 2 *Learn the following words*

verbs		nouns		adjective	
iuvat	he/she helps	**aqua**	water	**īrāta**	angry
laudat	he/she praises	**fābula**	story		
nārrat	he/she tells	**fīlia**	daughter	*adverb*	
parat	he/she prepares	**via**	road, way	**subitō**	suddenly
portat	he/she carries				
salūtat	he/she greets			*preposition*	
vocat	he/she calls			**in** + acc.	in, into

What is (a) an *irate* policeman? (b) a friendly *salutation*? (c) a long *narration*? (d) a *fabulous* animal? (e) What are *aquatic* sports? (f) What does a *porter* do?

From what Latin words are the words in italics derived?

What do the following sentences mean?

1 Horātia Scintillam vocat.
2 Scintilla puellam salūtat.
3 puella Scintillam iuvat.
4 fīliam laudat Scintilla. (Be careful!)

Argus steals the dinner

Read aloud, understand and translate the following story

Scintilla in casā labōrat; cēnam parat. fessa est. Horātia in viā cessat. Scintilla fīliam vocat. puella casam intrat et Scintillam iuvat; aquam in casam portat. Scintilla fīliam laudat.

cēna parāta est. Scintilla fīliam vocat et fābulam nārrat. Horātia
5 fābulam laeta audit. mox Argus casam intrat. cēnam spectat; subitō eam rapit et dēvorat. Scintilla īrāta est; Argus in viam fugit. Scintilla aliam cēnam parat.

in casā in the house
cessat is idling, hanging around

audit listens; **spectat** he looks at
eam rapit snatches it; **fugit** flees
aliam another

Respondē Latīnē (= answer in Latin)

1 quis (*who?*) cēnam parat?
2 quōmodo (*how?*) Horātia Scintillam iuvat?
3 quis casam intrat?
4 cūr (*why?*) Scintilla īrāta est? (**quod** = because)

WOMEN

Quintus' mother had to work extremely hard as the wife of a
Roman farmer. If the family were as poor as Horace says, she
lived in a house which probably consisted of just one room with a
hearth in the middle for the fire and a hole in the ceiling to let out
the smoke. She got up very early in the morning before it was
even light, stirred up the embers of last night's fire, and lit the
lamp. Then she began to spin and weave wool in order to make
clothes for her family and herself. She continued with this task
for most of the day. If she did have a daughter, she would of
course have used her help. They would have talked as they
worked at the wool, which would have made the long hours of
spinning and weaving pass more quickly. At some stage of the
day, Quintus' mother or sister had to go to the spring in the
middle of the town to fetch water. Here she would stop for a talk
with the local women before returning home with her full jar.

Women weaving

15

Quintus' mother may have prepared a simple breakfast for her husband before he went off to the country to his farm. She sent his lunch out to him as he worked in the fields and provided him with dinner, the largest meal of the day, when he returned home in the evening. On top of this, she had to see to all the housework and cope with the children. Her life was difficult and exhausting. Ancient Rome was very much a man's world, and the most important function of women was to produce children and bring up a new generation of Romans. While the main emphasis was on the boys, and a girl would not go to school after the primary stage, she could be taught at home by her mother or a gifted slave.

Marriages were arranged by the parents of the bride and bridegroom and often took place at a very early age. Marriage was legal for girls at twelve and for boys at fourteen, and most girls had become wives before their sixteenth birthday. Tullia, the daughter of Cicero, who is to enter our story later, was engaged at nine and when she died at the age of thirty she had been married three times. As with many marriages in non-Western cultures today, husband and wife might hardly have seen each other before the wedding. There is no reason to believe that this usually led to an unsuccessful marriage.

If the life of women in the Roman world sounds restricted and dull, it is worth reflecting that it was not unlike that of women in the Victorian era in Britain. This did not mean that women were downgraded or without influence. Couples expected to live in harmony with each other and many did. An inscription on one gravestone reads:

> To Urbana, the sweetest, chastest and rarest of wives, who certainly has never been surpassed, and deserves to be honoured for living with me to her last day in the greatest friendliness and simplicity. Her affection was matched by her industry. I added these words so that readers should understand how much we loved each other.

Another, set up by a freedman in Rome on the tomb of his wife, reads:

> This woman, who died before me, was my only wife; of chaste body, she loved me and was mistress of my heart; she lived faithful to her husband who was faithful to her, and never failed in her duty in any time of trouble.

Funeral monuments often show family groups in which husband and wife are represented with their children; the nuclear family was the norm, and most women found fulfilment in caring for their family. Nor was their work all dull. Weaving is a skilful and creative craft and managing a household a responsible and often a challenging job. The talking that women do together during these and other activities has often been dismissed as gossip: but women are also exchanging information, some of it very useful, and giving mutual support and practical help.

And women could by and large go where they wanted. Provided they were escorted by men (a slave would do), they could go to shops and temples and to the festivals and public entertainments which regularly took place. They were present at dinner parties with their husbands. In fact, despite the laws which restricted certain areas of their lives and which were gradually lifted in Horace's time, they did not live all that differently from other women in the Western world up to the women's liberation movement of the twentieth century.

Roman history is full of the names of women who made their mark because of their strong personalities. The women we know about came from the upper class, unlike Quintus' mother. Through her contacts, a politician's wife, mother or sister could have considerable influence. And many Roman women were well educated and witty. The household called their mistress 'domina' ('my lady') and she received visitors. At home she dined with her husband and she went out to dinner with him. Outside, she travelled in a litter, a portable couch enclosed by curtains, or walked with an attendant, and people made way for her in the street. Divorce was easy, even if one simply found one's partner irritating, and the fact that the husband had to give back her dowry with his divorced wife, put a wealthy woman in a strong position.

A woman having her hair dressed by a maidservant

The bachelor Quintus wrote: 'A wife with a dowry rules her husband.' What do you think he meant?

What seem to you the most striking differences between the position of women then and now? How would you like to have been a woman in the Roman world?

17

Chapter 3 — Quintus helps his father

Flaccus est colōnus Rōmānus. in agrō labōrat.

Flaccus Argum in agrum dūcit.

Argus Flaccum nōn iuvat sed dormit.

Quīntus agrum intrat. puer Argum vocat sed
Argus nōn audit; nam dormit.

This chapter introduces a new class of nouns with nominative ending **-us** or **-er**
(e.g. **colōnus**, **ager**, **puer**), accusative ending **-um** (e.g. **colōnum**, **agrum**, **puerum**).

Vocabulary 3

verbs		*nouns*		*pronoun*	
manet	he/she stays, waits	**terra**	earth, land	**eum** him, **eam** her (acc.)	
sedet	he/she sits	**cibus**	food		
videt	he/she sees	**colōnus**	farmer	*preposition*	
ascendit	he/she climbs	**fīlius**	son	**ad**	to, towards
cadit	he/she falls	**ager**	field		
currit	he/she runs	**puer**	boy, child	*conjunction*	
dūcit	he/she leads			**nam**	for
inquit	he/she says	*adjective*			
mittit	he/she sends	**ānxius, -a, -um** anxious			
redit	he/she returns				
audit	he/she hears				

Quintus helps his father

Read the following story aloud; understand and translate it

postrīdiē Scintilla Quīntum vocat; mittit eum ad agrum. Quīntus
cibum ad Flaccum portat; nam Flaccus diū in agrō labōrat et
fessus est. puer ad agrum festīnat; Argum sēcum dūcit. mox
Quīntus agrum intrat; Flaccum videt et vocat. Flaccus fīlium
5 audit et ad eum ambulat; in terrā sedet et cibum cōnsūmit.
  Quīntus domum nōn redit sed in agrō manet et Flaccum iuvat.
olīvam ascendit et olīvās dēcutit. Flaccus olīvās colligit. subitō
lāpsat Quīntus et ad terram cadit. Flaccus ānxius est et ad eum
currit, sed Quīntus nōn saucius est; surgit et domum redit.

postrīdiē the next day; **eum** him
diū for a long time
in agrō in the field
sēcum with him
in terrā on the ground
domum (to) home
olīvam olive tree; **olīvās** olives
dēcutit shakes down
colligit collects; **lāpsat** slips
saucius hurt; **surgit** gets up

Respondē Latīnē

1 cūr (*why?*) Quīntus in agrō manet?
    (**quod** = because)
2 quōmodo (*how?*) Quīntus Flaccum iuvat?
3 cūr ānxius est Flaccus?

Read through the Latin passage above once
more. See how many Latin words you can find
which have English derivatives (i.e. English
words which come from the Latin words).
Write down each Latin word together with its
English derivative (you should be able to find
at least ten).

Gathering olives

Flaccus Quīntum laudat

Translate the first paragraph of the passage below and answer the questions on the second paragraph without translating

Quīntus domum redit et Scintillam salūtat; Argum in hortum dūcit et Horātiam vocat. Horātia in hortum festīnat; laeta est quod Quīntus adest.

5   Flaccus ab agrō redit; fessus est; in casā sedet et quiēscit. mox 'Quīntus' inquit 'puer bonus est. in agrō manet et mē iuvat.' Scintilla laeta est, quod Flaccus puerum laudat. cēnam celeriter parat; ubi parāta est cēna, Horātiam et Quīntum in casam vocat. Quīntus laetus est quod cēna parāta est; in casam festīnat.

1	What does Flaccus do when he returns?	[3]
2	Why is Scintilla glad?	[2]
3	Why is Quintus glad?	[2]
4	In what case is each of the following words:	

      Scintillam (line 1)
      laeta (line 6)
      puerum (line 6)
      casam (line 7)?

    Explain why these cases are used.   [8]

domum home; **hortum** garden
quod because
adest is there
ab agrō from the field
quiēscit rests; **bonus** good; **mē** me
celeriter quickly
ubi when

A slave sale

SLAVES AND FREEDMEN

Slavery is a terrible thing, but before we make too harsh judgements on the past, we should remember that it was not abolished in Britain until 1833 or in the USA until 1863. Up till the eighteenth century it was taken for granted.

Who were slaves? Many of them had been defeated in a war and their conquerors could have killed them. Therefore they – and their children – were supposed to feel gratitude to their conquerors, and it seemed fitting that they had no rights at all. But in fact slaves came from other sources too. Many were the victims of kidnapping or piracy; many were unwanted children who had either been left out to die by their parents when new-born and then rescued, or been sold off to slave-traders when they were older. Slavery was big business and it is said that at one of its main centres, the Greek island of Delos, 20,000 slaves were sold in a day.

What was it like to be a slave? If you had to row in the galleys or work in the mines or quarries, life was very unpleasant indeed. Literate and intelligent slaves had some chance of avoiding these fates. The best situation was to be born in a household where you might be treated up to a point as one of the family, for the Roman *familia* included the slaves and so they felt that they belonged somewhere. But legally slaves had no individual rights. Masters gave them their names and addressed the males as '*puer*'. They could punish without any fear of the law and they could be very savage. Vedius Pollio ordered a boy who had broken a valuable crystal cup to be executed by being thrown to the lampreys in his fishpond. The emperor Hadrian flew into a rage with his secretary and poked out his eye with a pen. The authors who tell us these things disapproved of them, but they happened. Beating was considered a perfectly acceptable punishment, and Cato the Elder recommended that sick and old slaves should be sold off, not kept on unproductively.

However appalling their lot, it remains true that many slaves did owe their lives to those who had enslaved them, and slaves and freedmen often gave each other emotional support. But their situation was extremely insecure. They could be beaten, sold or killed.

Generally they would suppress their own personalities and do anything to please their masters. However, many masters realized that the best way to persuade their slaves to work hard and be loyal was to show them kindness. Everything a slave owned really belonged to his master, but many Romans encouraged their slaves by letting them keep any money they saved. Thus it was often possible for slaves to build up enough money to buy their freedom from their masters. The sum of money was called the *pecūlium* and the master could use it to buy a new, younger slave. In addition, masters could reward excellent service from slaves by giving them their freedom even without payment, either while the masters were alive or in their wills. In fact almost all slaves who had a reasonably close relationship with their master could expect to be set free quite soon.

And some masters treated their slaves very well. The philosopher Seneca wrote to a friend:

> I am delighted to discover from some people who have come from seeing you that you live on friendly terms with your slaves. This is what I should have expected of your good sense and your learning. People say, 'They are slaves.' I disagree. They are men. 'They are slaves,' they say. No, they are people you share your house with. 'They are slaves.' No, they are humble friends. 'They are slaves.' No, they are fellow-slaves if you consider how much power fortune has over both slaves and free alike... Consider that the man you call a slave is born from the same species as yourself, enjoys the same sky, and lives, breathes and dies just as you do.

Though slaves won Roman citizenship with their freedom, they were expected to show obedience and loyalty to their former owner, who became their 'patron' instead of their 'master'. Most freedmen lived humble lives but some gained considerable money, power and influence.

Relations between patrons and freedmen were often close. Cicero's freedman Tiro became his indispensable private secretary and Cicero's letters to Tiro when the latter was ill show a deep concern for him; Cicero's son Marcus wrote to him as 'my dearest Tiro' and treated him as an old and respected family friend.

A Roman novel, the *Satyricon* of Petronius, depicts a freedman who had become a millionaire and lived a most extravagant and ostentatious life. Inscriptions on tombs show that many freedmen were successful in various professions. An inscription from Assisi records the career of P. Decimius Eros Merula, the freedman of Publius, who was a physician, a surgeon and an oculist. He bought his freedom for 50,000 sesterces (a very large sum); he gave 20,000 to become a priest of Augustus, the one public office a freedman might hold; he gave large sums to set up statues in the temple of Hercules and even larger sums for paving the public

Two freedmen, one of them a blacksmith, the other a carpenter. You can see the tools of their trade at the top and on the right.

streets, and he left a considerable fortune. He was clearly a talented and public spirited citizen of Assisi who led a successful and fulfilled life. The civil service instituted by Augustus contained many talented freedmen who gradually became the most powerful servants of the state.

The sons of freedmen were full citizens who could hold any public office. It is probably true that within a century of Horace's death there were more citizens descended from freedmen than from the original Roman population. The poet Juvenal, who hated foreigners, wrote this in about 100 AD: 'The Orontes [a river in Syria] has long ago flooded into the Tiber', by which he meant that pure Roman stock had long been diluted by Eastern blood. Despite the racism of this comment, the fact remains that the Romans gave their citizenship to all races in their empire.

The following inscription on a tomb tells in brief the story of the rather sad life of a freedman who was born free in Parthia, the great kingdom to the east of the Roman empire, and ended his life as a Roman citizen in Ravenna in north-east Italy:

C. Julius Mygdonius, a Parthian by race, born free, captured in youth and sold into Roman territory. When I became a Roman citizen by the help of fate, I saved up my money for the day I should be fifty. From my youth onwards I longed to reach old age. Now, tomb, receive me gladly. With you I shall be free from care.

Basing your answer on the information in this essay, write an imaginary life story of a freedman in the Roman world.

23

puer puellam videt; eam vocat.

puerī puellās vident; eās vocant.

puella puerum audit et respondet.

puellae puerōs audiunt et respondent.

Argus bonus est.

Argus et Fīdus malī sunt.

Latin distinguishes between *singular* (one person or thing)
and *plural* (more than one) by changing word endings.
This applies to verbs, nouns and adjectives.

Vocabulary 4

verbs		*adverbs*		*nouns*	
adest	he/she is present	**cūr?**	why?	**amīcus**	friend
cūrat	he/she cares, looks after	**diū**	for a long time	**lūdus**	school
accēdit	he/she approaches	**iam**	now, already		
prōcēdit	he/she goes forward	**lentē**	slowly	*pronouns*	
surgit	he/she rises	**saepe**	often	**eōs, eās**	them (acc. pl.)
dormit	he/she sleeps	**tandem**	at last	**ille, illa**	he, she
venit	he/she comes				

adjectives		*conjunctions*	
magnus, -a, -um	great, big	**quod**	because
miser, misera, miserum	miserable	**ubi**	when
multus, -a, -um	much, many		

Scintilla and Horatia at the fountain

Read aloud, understand and translate the following story

cotīdiē ubi Flaccus ad agrum prōcēdit, Scintilla et Horātia ad
fontem festīnant. magnās urnās portant. ubi ad fontem veniunt,
multae fēminae iam adsunt. aliae aquam dūcunt, aliae urnās
plēnās portant. Scintilla eās salūtat et diū colloquium cum amīcīs
5 facit. Horātia cum puellīs lūdit. tandem Scintilla aquam dūcit et
domum redit. Horātia quoque aquam dūcit et post Scintillam
festīnat.

urna magna est; Horātia eam aegrē portat. subitō lāpsat; urna
ad terram cadit; aqua in terram effluit. Horātia in terrā sedet;
10 'heu, heu,' inquit; 'urna frācta est.' Scintillam vocat; illa redit et 'ō
fīlia,' inquit, 'cūr in terrā sedēs? surge* et aliam urnam ā casā
portā*.' Horātia surgit; ad casam redit et aliam urnam ad fontem
portat. aquam dūcit et domum festīnat.

ubi Horātia domum redit, Quīntus iam ad lūdum prōcēdit.
15 lentē ambulat et saepe cōnsistit. Horātia festīnat et mox eum
videt. 'manē*, Quīnte,' inquit. manet Quīntus; Horātia ad eum
currit. ad lūdum ūnā prōcēdunt.

cotīdiē every day
fontem the spring; **urnās** water pots
aliae ... aliae some ... others
dūcunt draw; **plēnās** full
colloquium ... facit makes
  conversation, chats
cum amīcīs with her friends
lūdit plays; **domum** (to) home
quoque also; **post** after
aegrē with difficulty; **lāpsat** slips
effluit flows out
heu, heu! alas, alas!; **frācta** broken
ā casā from the house

cōnsistit stops

ūnā together

*NB **surge** (get up!), **portā** (carry!) **manē** (wait!): these verbs
are in the imperative form, the part of the verb used to give
orders; it is explained in chapter 8.

A scene from twentieth-century Italy

Women filling urns at the spring

Respondē Latīnē

1 cūr Horātia urnam aegrē (*with difficulty*) portat?
2 quōmodo (*how?*) Horātia urnam frangit (*breaks*)?
3 cūr Horātia ad casam redit?

Flaccus goes to the pub

Translate the first paragraph of the following passage and answer the questions below on the second paragraph

ubi cēna cōnfecta est, Flaccus in viam exit et ad tabernam ambulat. ubi tabernam intrat, multōs amīcōs videt. illī eum salūtant. Flaccus sedet et vīnum bibit.

amīcī colloquium diū faciunt; miserī sunt; multās querēlās
5 faciunt. Seleucus 'heu, heu,' inquit; 'diū nōn pluit; agrī siccī sunt.' Chrȳsanthus 'cibus cārus est,' inquit; 'colōnī miserī sunt, sed nēmō eōs iuvat.' Philērus 'duovirī' inquit 'colōnōs nōn cūrant.' aliī aliās querēlās faciunt. sed Flaccus eōs nōn audit; fessus est; interdum dormit, interdum vīnum bibit. tandem surgit
10 et domum redit.

1 How are Flaccus' friends feeling?   [2]
2 What do they complain about?   [6]
3 How does Flaccus react to their talk?   [4]

cōnfecta finished; **exit** goes out
tabernam the pub
vīnum wine
colloquium faciunt make
    conversation, talk
querēlās complaints
pluit it has rained; **siccī** dry
cārus dear, expensive
nēmō no one; **duovirī** the magistrates
aliī others; **interdum** sometimes
domum (to) home

THE COUNTRY TOWN: VENUSIA

In the beginning, Rome was not the capital of Italy. It was the home of a small tribe which often had to fight for its survival with the other Italian peoples. However, Rome defeated and made alliances with its rivals, and, long before Horace's time, had become the leading city of Italy.

The Romans used one especially successful method to build up and keep their power. They sent out Roman citizens to found or settle in towns in various parts of Italy. This meant that they could spread their influence and look after their interests. Later, when the population of Rome became too great, the problem could be eased by sending out the overflow of citizens to create such settlements. In the same way, when Roman soldiers finished their military service and had to be discharged with a pension, they could be sent to settle in new or captured towns.

These towns were called *colōniae*, and Quintus' home-town Venusia was one of them.* *Colōnus* is the Latin for a smallholder – a farmer, such as Quintus' father, who worked only a little land – and the word *colōnia* shows us that when they left the army the soldiers turned their hand to farming. In 261 BC a large number of Roman colonists were sent to settle in Venusia. They were joined by a further group in 200 BC. With its situation on the Appian Way, Italy's principal road – which made it a customary stopping-off place – it was a large and important town with its own forum, senate house, law courts, temples, gymnasium, amphitheatre and baths. Only a few remains of the last two survive and our illustrations are of Pompeii, another colony in Southern Italy perhaps similar in size. This was a lively and civilized city. The streets were paved, and the ruts made by the endless wheels of wagons and chariots can still be seen. So too can the stepping stones helpfully positioned to get pedestrians across without treading in the filth below. There are fountains on many of the corners, and many bars along the streets, welcome sources of coolness and refreshment in the intense southern heat.

(* In Britain there were colonies at Colchester, Lincoln, Gloucester and York.)

Stepping stones across a paved street in Pompeii

Above: The Forum and
Temple of Jupiter at Pompeii

Right:
A tavern
at Pompeii

Below: An election poster

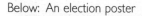

The original settlers of a colony and their descendants kept their Roman citizenship and the colony was organized on the model of Rome itself. There were annual elections – hotly contested, as you will see in Part II (chapter 17) – of the *duovirī* ('two men') to preside over the local senate (council) just as the two consuls, the chief men at Rome, were elected every year to preside over the government in the capital. The idea was that by having two people in charge one of them could check the other's foolish or dangerous intentions. In addition, the colonies had their own priests. The first colonies were in Italy, but later they were founded throughout the Roman empire. The *colōnī* were envied and respected by their neighbours because they were Roman citizens.

The *colōnia* covered a large area of land, which had been given to it when the land was taken away from the original inhabitants at its foundation. Thus it included both town and country and so its inhabitants were not only the townsfolk who provided various services – with such trades as bakers and wine-merchants forming guilds – but also farmers; many of these farmers would have lived in the town and trudged out to their farms. Quintus' father fell into both categories. As well as being a farmer, he had a town job as an auctioneer's agent.

Quintus tells us that the original settlers in Venusia had been sent to keep the peace in a remote and violent part of Italy. The local schoolmaster was Flavius and it was to his school, Quintus tells us, that 'boys who were the descendants of big centurions used to go, their satchels and tablets hung from their left shoulders'. It did not strike his father as a suitable place to send his son. Probably Quintus was simply too intelligent. So his father took him off to Rome to be educated.

Quintus' friend and fellow poet Virgil writes of Italian towns 'piled up on cliff tops with rivers flowing beneath their ancient walls'. Such hill towns remain a feature of the Italian landscape and even today, when viewed from a distance, they probably look much the same as in Quintus' time.

An Italian hill town

What similarities can you find between Venusia and/or Pompeii and a modern country town?

Quīntus amīcum rogat: 'cūr in agrō labōrās?'
amīcus respondet: 'colōnum iuvō.'

Quīntus amīcōs rogat: 'cūr in agrō labōrātis?'
amīcī respondent: 'colōnōs iuvāmus.'

Scintilla Quīntum rogat: 'cūr in terrā iacēs, Quīnte?'
Quīntus respondet: 'in terrā iaceō, quod fessus sum.'

Quīntus puellās rogat: 'cūr in hortō sedētis, puellae?'
puellae respondent: 'in hortō sedēmus, quod fessae sumus.'

Quīntus Scintillam rogat: 'quid facis?'
Scintilla respondet: 'cēnam parō.'

Horātia puerōs rogat: 'quid facitis, puerī?'
puerī respondent: 'ad lūdum festīnāmus.'

Note the changes in verb endings which show what 'person' the subject is: I, you (singular), he/she, we, you (plural), they.

Vocabulary 5

verbs		noun		pronoun	
clāmat	he/she shouts	**hortus**	garden	**quid?**	what?
dat	he/she gives				
rogat	he/she asks	*adjectives*		*prepositions*	
spectat	he/she watches	**ūnus, -a, -um**	one	**cum** + abl.	with
iacet	he/she lies (down)	**duo, duae, duo**	two	**in** + abl.	in, on
respondet	he/she answers	**trēs, tria**	three	**per** + acc.	through,
dīcit	he/she says	**alius, alia,**			throughout
emit	he/she buys	**aliud**	other, another		
pōnit	he/she places, puts	**bonus, -a, -um**	good	*conjunction*	
trādit	he/she hands over	**malus, -a, -um**	bad	**nec/neque**	and not, nor
advenit	he/she arrives				
facit	he/she makes,	*adverb*			
	he/she does	**statim**	at once		

Market day

postrīdiē Flaccus et Scintilla māne surgunt; nam nūndinae sunt.
Flaccus magnum saccum lānae portat; Scintilla olīvās et fīcōs in
calathōs pōnit. Horātia in hortō sedet. mox Scintilla Horātiam
vocat; 'quid facis, Horātia?' inquit; 'parāta es? ad forum
5 prōcēdimus.' Horātia respondet: 'parāta sum; veniō statim.'
Flaccus lānam portat, Scintilla olīvās, Horātia fīcōs; festīnant ad
forum.

   ubi ad forum adveniunt, multī virī et fēminae iam adsunt; per
tōtum forum tabernae sunt. colōnī clāmant et mercēs suās
10 laudant. aliī ūvās vendunt, aliī lānam, aliī fīcōs. Flaccus
Scintillam et fīliam dūcit ad locum vacuum; tabernam ērigunt et
mercēs expōnunt.

   mox amīcus ad tabernam accēdit et Flaccum salūtat; lānam
spectat. Flaccus 'lāna bona est' inquit 'nec cāra. tōtum saccum
15 tribus dēnāriīs vendō.' amīcus 'nimium rogās, Flacce,' inquit;
'duōs dēnāriōs dō.' Flaccus concēdit et saccum trādit.

   intereā fēmina ad Scintillam accēdit et 'quantī' rogat 'olīvae
sunt?' illa respondet: 'illās olīvās ūnō dēnāriō vendō.' fēmina
olīvās emit. alia fēmina accēdit et fīcōs diū spectat; Horātia rogat
20 'cūr fīcōs sīc spectās?' illa 'illōs fīcōs sīc spectō,' inquit 'quod
malī sunt.' Horātia īrāta est et respondet: 'quid dīcis? malōs fīcōs
nōn vendimus. fīcī bonī sunt.' sed fēmina fīcōs nōn emit.

   mox omnēs mercēs vendunt. Scintilla laeta est; 'omnēs mercēs
vendidimus,' inquit; 'iam ad tabernam piscātōriam prōcēdō.'

postrīdiē the next day; **māne** early
nūndinae sunt it is market day
saccum lānae sack of wool
fīcōs figs; **calathōs** baskets
forum city centre, market place

tōtum whole
tabernae sunt there are stalls
mercēs suās their wares
ūvās grapes; **vendunt** are selling
locum vacuum an empty place
ērigunt put up; **expōnunt** put out
cāra dear, expensive
tribus dēnāriīs for three denarii
vendō I am selling; **nimium** too much
concēdit agrees; **trādit** hands over
intereā meanwhile;
quantī? how much?
sīc thus, like that

omnēs mercēs all their wares
vendidimus we have sold
tabernam piscātōriam the fish stall

31

Word-building

It is often possible to guess the meaning of Latin words from the English words which come from them. What do the following Latin words mean?

Shopping in an Italian market today

verbs	nouns	adjectives
dēfendō	familia	ānxius
dēscendō	flamma	dēsertus
repellō	glōria	dīvīnus
resistō	memōria	timidus

(Since many words can easily be guessed from their similarity to English words, e.g. **cōnsūm-ō** = I consume, eat; **dēvor-ō** = I devour, we do not always gloss them in the passages. But all such words are included in the General Vocabulary.)

Fābella: To the fish stall

Persōnae: **Scintilla, Flaccus, Horātia, Piscātor**

    Scintilla Flaccum et fīliam ad tabernam piscātōriam dūcit.

Flaccus: quid facis, Scintilla? quō festīnās? piscēs cārī sunt.

Scintilla: bonam cēnam emō. piscēs nōn valdē cārī sunt.

5   *Flaccus ad tabernam accēdit et piscēs diū spectat.*

Piscātor: quid facis? cūr piscēs sīc spectās?

Flaccus: piscēs malī sunt, piscātor; olent.

Piscātor: quid dīcis? nōn olent piscēs; bonī sunt.

Scintilla: tacē, Flacce. piscēs nōn olent. piscātor, quantī sunt

10   hī piscēs?

Piscātor: illōs piscēs ūnō dēnāriō vendō.

Horātia: nimium rogās, piscātor.

Scintilla: tacē, Horātia. nōn nimium rogat. piscēs emō.

    Scintilla ūnum dēnārium trādit et piscēs accipit.

15   **Horātia:**   iam domum prōcēdimus? ego iēiūna sum.

Scintilla: domum prōcēdimus. mox bene cēnābimus.

Flaccus: bene cēnābimus, sed quam cāra erit illa cēna!

persōnae characters
piscātor fisherman

quō? where to?; **piscēs** fish
valdē very

olent smell

tacē be quiet!; **quantī**? how much?
hī these

nimium too much

trādit hands over; **accipit** receives

domum home; **iēiūna** starving
bene cēnābimus we shall dine well
quam cāra how expensive!
erit will be

Fish mosaic

33

THE ROMAN FARMER – AND MARKET DAY

Quintus' early years in Venusia left him with a deep love for the country. After he had become a successful poet in Rome, he was overjoyed to be given a small estate in the Sabine Hills to the north-east of the city. Here he would entertain his guests with vegetarian dinners suitable for the simple country life.

Quintus had eight slaves to run his Sabine farm. For his father, on the other hand, life would have been extremely hard. He would have grown enough food to keep his family alive, living in a humble cottage in Venusia and tramping out to the country every day to work on his farm as some peasants still do in modern Italy. Here he would have worked for most of the daylight hours through almost all of the year. The lists of farmers' tasks in Roman times show a break in the middle of the winter which lasted only a month. The summer drought may have allowed them some time off as well, though if it was possible to irrigate the land, that would have to be seen to.

Flaccus grew olives, vines, grain and vegetables on his farm. Oil from the olives provided the fuel for lamps and was used in soap and cooking, as in Mediterranean countries today. The vines produced wine, the grapes being trampled underfoot to extract the juice. Italy was also famous for honey and he may well have kept bees.

Two farmers' calendars survive from Rome, and here are the lists of jobs for May and September from one of them:

Treading grapes to extract the juice for winemaking

MAY	SEPTEMBER
Weed corn	*Treat wine jars with pitch*
Shear sheep	*Pick apples*
Wash wool	*Loosen earth round roots of trees*
Break in young bullocks	*Feast in honour of Minerva*
Cut vetch (a legume)	
Bless the cornfields	
Sacrifice to Mercury and Flora	

The Romans always expressed the highest admiration for the simple country life, though they were more enthusiastic about praising it than living it! Virgil writes of an old pirate from Cilicia in Asia who had ended up farming in Southern Italy. He 'had a few acres of left-over land, and this a soil not fertile enough for bullocks to plough, not right for sheep and not suitable for vines. But he planted herbs here and there amid the thickets, and white lillies round about, and vervain, and the slender poppy, and matched in contentment the wealth of kings. Returning home late at night, he would pile his table with a feast for which he had paid nothing.' (How far can you believe this? Is it too good to be true?) For the Romans, farming stood for the qualities of tough simplicity that had made their nation great. One of their greatest heroes was a modest farmer, Cincinnatus, who was called from the plough to save the state, and, after defeating the enemy, at once went back to finish his ploughing (see chapter 15 below).

Poultry and fruit being sold in a Roman market

Every eighth day there were market days. These were called *nūndinae* ('ninth-day affairs'), because of the Romans' inclusive way of counting (1+7+1). After seven days of hard work, people smartened themselves up and hurried to the market with their families. *Nūndinae* were regular school holidays, eagerly looked forward to by the children. The farmers would bring their produce to town to sell it to the townspeople and go home with money and tools for their farms, while their wives might buy pots and pans etc. A number of farmers would have lived in outlying villages and farms. Virgil writes of one of these, a peasant called Simylus who grew cabbages, beet, sorrel, mallow and radishes for sale: 'Every market day he carried on his shoulder bundles of produce for sale to the city; and returned home from there, his neck relieved of its burden, but his pocket heavy with money.' Market day was also a good chance to visit a lawyer and do some business. And the townsmen might entertain some of their friends from the country at a celebratory lunch.

At the time when our story is set, Italy contained many vast country estates. On these, large-scale agricultural enterprises such as cattle ranching and the cultivation of vines and olives would be carried out. A fabulously wealthy freedman called Caecilius Metellus had 4,116 slaves on his estate. Many slaves who worked on such estates had a grim life. When not engaged in backbreaking work in chain gangs, they were housed in dreadful barracks. The only aim was to bring in as much money as possible for the usually absentee owners. An ancient writer called Varro talks about three types of farm equipment: 'the kind that speaks (i.e. slaves), the kind that cannot speak (i.e. cattle) and the voiceless (i.e. agricultural tools)'. These huge estates, which used slaves as machines, had originally caused massive unemployment among the peasant farmers. But by Horace's day slave labour had become more expensive and the *colōnus* had made a comeback. Alongside the vast estates there were smallholdings of just a few hectares, and it was one of these that Horace's father worked.

Describe the farming operations illustrated in this picture. How do they resemble or differ from farming methods today?

pŭerī et puellae prope iānuam manent. magister
eōs iubet intrāre et sedēre.

(handwritten annotations: near the door; here & orders)

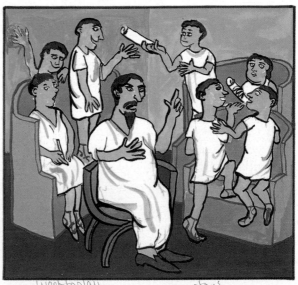

pŭerī lūdere cŭpiunt. magister dīcit: 'labōrāre
dēbētis.'

(handwritten annotations: want to play; stays; you must work)

Decimus litterās male scrībit; magister eum
iubet litterās iterum scrībere.

(handwritten annotation: again)

tandem pŭerī dīligenter labōrant; magister
cōnstituit fābulam nārrāre.

(handwritten annotations: hard; decides)

Another part of the verb, the infinitive, is here introduced, e.g. **intrā-re** = to enter, **sedē-re** = to sit.

pŭerī: besides meaning 'boys', this word in the plural can mean 'children', 'boys and girls'.
When masculine and feminine are paired together, e.g. 'boys and girls', their gender is treated as
masculine, e.g. **pŭerī et puellae fessī sunt**.

Vocabulary 6

NB From now on in the vocabularies, verbs are given with their infinitives; these show to which conjugation each verb belongs, e.g. **festīnō**, **festīnāre**: *1st conjugation* (like **parō**, **parāre**); **doceō**, **docēre**: *2nd conjugation* (like **moneō**, **monēre**); **lūdō**, **lūdere**: *3rd conjugation* (like **regō**, **regere**); **dormiō**, **dormīre**: *4th conjugation* (like **audiō**, **audīre**); **cupiō**, **cupere**: *mixed conjugation* (like **capiō**, **capere**)

verbs

dēbeō, dēbēre	I ought, I must		
doceō, docēre	I teach		
iubeō, iubēre	I order		
cōnstituō, cōnstituere	I decide		
dīmittō, dīmittere	I send away		
lūdō, lūdere	I play		
scrībō, scrībere	I write		
cupiō, cupere	I desire, I want		
eō, īre	I go		
exeō, exīre	I go out		

adjectives

cēterī, cēterae, cētera	the others, the rest
meus, -a, -um	my
tuus, -a, -um	your

nouns

iānua	door
littera	a letter
domus	home
domum (to) home	
magister	master

pronouns

ego I, **mē** (acc.) me
tū you, **tē** (acc.) you

adverbs

celeriter	quickly
dīligenter	carefully, hard
iterum	again

preposition

prope + acc.   near

conjunctions

itaque   and so
nec/neque ... nec/neque   neither ... nor

The school of Flavius

Quīntus ad lūdum lentē ambulat et saepe cōnsistit, sed Horātia celeriter prōcēdit; prior ad lūdum advenit et puellās salūtat quae prope iānuam manent; longum colloquium cum Iūliā facit, puellā valdē pulchrā. Quīntus in viā amīcum videt, nōmine Gāium; eum
5 vocat. Gāius ad lūdum festīnat sed ubi Quīntum audit, cōnsistit et 'quid facis, Quīnte?' inquit; 'festīnāre dēbēs. sērō ad lūdum venīs. ego festīnō.' Quīntus respondet: 'nōn sērō venīmus, Gāī.' Gāium iubet manēre. ille ānxius est sed manet. itaque Quīntus et Gāius lentē ad lūdum prōcēdunt.

cōnsistit stops
prior first; **quae** who
colloquium talk, conversation
pulchrā pretty
nōmine by name, called
sērō late

magister clamat:
'cur sero venis?
malus puer es!'

10   cēterī puerī iam adsunt. magister ē iānuā exit et eōs iubet   **ē** out of
intrāre et sedēre; puerī lūdere cupiunt, puellae labōrāre. magister
ubi nec Quīntum nec Gāium videt, īrātus est et clāmat: 'cūr nōn
adsunt Quīntus et Gāius? cūr sērō veniunt?' tandem intrant
Quīntus et Gāius et magistrum salūtant. sed ille clāmat: 'cūr sērō
15 venītis? malī puerī estis.' iubet eōs celeriter sedēre.
    diū sedent puerī et magistrum audiunt; diū clāmat magister et
litterās docet. puerī litterās in tabulīs scrībunt; magister tabulās   **tabulīs** tablets
spectat et litterās corrigit.   **corrigit** corrects
    Decimus, puer magnus et stultus, litterās aegrē discit. magister   **stultus** foolish
20 eum iubet tabulam ad sē ferre; tabulam spectat. 'Decime,' inquit,   **aegrē discit** learns with difficulty
'asinus es; litterās nōn rēctē scrībis.' Decimus 'errās, magister,'   **ad sē ferre** to bring to him
inquit; 'asinus nōn sum. litterās rēctē scrībō. ecce!' litterās iterum   **rēctē** rightly, correctly
scrībit. sed Flāvius 'impudēns es, Decime,' inquit 'et asinus;   **errās** you are wrong; **ecce** look!
litterās nōn rēctē scrībis.'
25   diū labōrant puerī. tandem Iūlia 'dīligenter labōrāmus,
magister,' inquit; 'litterās bene scrībimus; fessī sumus. itaque   **bene** well
dēbēs nōs domum dīmittere.'
    Flāvius eam benignē spectat. 'ita vērō,' inquit; 'dīligenter   **benignē** kindly; **ita vērō** yes
labōrātis, puerī. itaque vōs iubeō domum abīre.' cēterī laetī   **abīre** to go away
30 domum festīnant, sed Flāvius Decimum iubet in lūdō manēre. 'tū,
Decime,' inquit, 'dēbēs litterās iterum scrībere.' itaque Decimus
in lūdō miser sedet dum cēterī in viā lūdunt.   **dum** while

Writing implements

39

Respondē Latīnē

1 cūr prior (*first*) ad lūdum advenit Horātia?
2 ubi Quīntus et Gāius adveniunt, cūr īrātus est magister?
3 cūr dīcit magister: 'Decime, asinus es'?
4 quid respondet Decimus?

Flavius decides to tell a story

Translate the first paragraph of the passage below and answer the questions on the second paragraph without translating

postrīdiē Quīntus et Horātia et Gāius mātūrē ad lūdum adveniunt, sed Decimus sērō advenit. Flāvius 'cūr sērō ad lūdum venīs, Decime?' inquit. Decimus respondet: 'errās, magister. ego nōn sērō veniō. cēterī mātūrius adveniunt.' Flāvius valdē īrātus est;

5 'impudēns es, Decime,' inquit; iubet eum sedēre et dīligenter labōrāre.

    mox puerī litterās scrībunt. dīligenter labōrant. tandem Horātia 'magister,' inquit, 'dīligenter labōrāmus et litterās diū scrībimus. fessī sumus. itaque dēbēs fābulam nōbīs nārrāre.'

10 Flāvius 'ita vērō,' inquit, 'dīligenter labōrātis. quod bonī puerī estis, volō fābulam nārrāre.' iubet eōs attendere et sē audīre.

postrīdiē the next day; **mātūrē** early
sērō late

mātūrius too early

nōbīs (to) us
ita vērō yes
volō I'm willing; **sē** him

1 What do the children do when the lesson starts? [3]
2 What does Horatia ask Flavius to do, and why? [3]
3 Why does Flavius agree to her request? [2]

EDUCATION

Most Roman citizens were literate and their children received a primary education at the local schools from the ages of six or seven to eleven or twelve. Here they were taught reading, writing and elementary arithmetic. The evidence suggests that girls as well as boys attended these schools, though they did not, at far as we know, go on to the secondary or 'grammar' schools. In our story we make both Quintus and Horatia go to the school of Flavius for their primary education but his father takes the boy away to Rome for his secondary education.

    A wealthy family would appoint a slave, often a Greek, as a kind of personal tutor who would take a child to and from school. He might also act as a language assistant in Greek (see below). The two of them would be accompanied by another slave who carried the child's books. In country towns, schoolchildren went to school on their own carrying their satchels and taking along the schoolmaster's pay once a month. But when Quintus went to school in Rome, his father took him there and sat in on his lessons.

In primary education, i.e. the first three or four years, the three 'R's were hammered into boys and girls with a syllabus of reading and writing in both Latin and Greek. The pupils would write their lessons on tablets (*tabulae*) using a stylus. They would also learn elementary arithmetic using an abacus. Horace poked fun at maths lessons in his poetry:

> Roman boys learn how to divide a penny by a hundred with long calculations. 'Tell us, son of Albinus, what do you end up with if a twelfth is taken away from five twelfths? Can you say?' 'A third.' 'Well done! You'll end up a millionaire. What does it come to if you add a twelfth?' 'A half.' Is it any surprise that when we drag our children through these off-putting financial calculations they can't find the inspiration for poetry?

For the most part, the lessons were boring and unpleasant. Pupils sat on uncomfortable benches or chairs, often in noisy surroundings. They endlessly recited the alphabet both forwards and backwards, as well as chanting their multiplication tables again and again. Teaching started very early, soon after dawn, and a Roman poet called Martial complained violently at being woken up by the noise:

> Why can't you stay out of our lives, you cursed schoolmaster, a man hateful to boys and girls alike? The crested cocks have not yet broken the silence of the night. Already you are making a noise with your cruel voice and your thwacks.

After a break for lunch lessons probably started up again. There would be a holiday every eighth day, short breaks in the winter and spring, and a very long holiday in the summer.

Scenes in a boy's education

Boys would move on to another school around the age of eleven or twelve for their secondary education. Here they would learn grammar or literature. Greek and Greek literature were an important part of the syllabus. All educated Romans were bilingual. Though they had conquered Greece, they still recognized the greatness of Greek literature. As Horace himself wrote, 'Conquered Greece conquered its wild conqueror and brought the arts to rustic Italy.'

At the secondary stage arithmetic, geometry, music and astronomy were studied as minor subjects. The curriculum was not wide. There were medical schools in Greece but in Italy there was no scientific education at all. When they were about sixteen, upper-class Roman boys went on for their tertiary education to a teacher of rhetoric who would teach them through public lectures. From him they received a thorough training in speaking and arguing, and this was a good preparation for a career in politics (see Part II, chapter 24).

After girls had dropped out of education at school after the first (primary) stage, they learnt needlework, dancing, singing and lyre-playing at home.

What are the similarities and the differences between the education that you are receiving and what you would have been taught in a Roman school?

The Roman writer Pliny the Younger summed up a good school. It should have admirable teaching, firm discipline and high standards of behaviour. He thought that forming the character was as important as training the mind. What do you think?

The Romans themselves were puzzled that lūdus, *the Latin word for school, also means a game. One writer thought that the word might have been chosen to lead children to believe that school was more fun than it actually was. It is also possible that the term comes from a time when games, PE, were the basis of Roman education. What do you think?*

Quīntus canem in agrum dūcit et patrem salūtat.

pater et fīlius ab agrō cum cane domum redeunt.

in viā Quīntus multōs comitēs videt; illī omnēs eum salūtant.

pater canem domum dūcit, sed Quīntus cum comitibus lūdit.

Note that a new type of noun appears in these captions; what are the endings of these nouns for (a) accusative singular, (b) accusative plural, (c) ablative singular, (d) ablative plural?

Vocabulary 7

From now on the vocabularies list nouns with nominative, genitive (= 'of'; see chapter 9) and gender, e.g.

1st declension: **fīlia, fīliae**, f. daughter (*this is abbreviated to*: **fīlia, -ae**, f. daughter)
2nd declension: **fīlius, fīliī**, m. son (*abbreviated to*: **fīlius, -ī**, m. son)
3rd declension: **rēx, rēgis**, m. king (*the genitives of 3rd declension nouns are not abbreviated*)

Some nouns can by sense be either masculine or feminine, e.g. **comes** = a male or a female companion; *their genders are given as* c. = common. *3rd declension adjectives are given in two forms, e.g.* **fortis** *(masculine and feminine),* **forte** *(neuter)*

verbs		*nouns*	
convocō, convocāre	I call together	**īra, -ae**, f.	anger
nāvigō, nāvigāre	I sail	**pugna, -ae**, f.	fight
oppugnō, oppugnāre	I attack	**canis, canis**, c.	dog
pugnō, pugnāre	I fight	**comes, comitis**, c.	comrade
dēfendō, dēfendere	I defend	**frāter, frātris**, m.	brother
occīdō, occīdere	I kill	**nāvis, nāvis**, f.	ship
resistō, resistere	I resist	**pater, patris**, m.	father
vincō, vincere	I conquer	**prīnceps, prīncipis**, m.	prince
capiō, capere*	I take	**rēx, rēgis**, m.	king
fugiō, fugere*	I flee	**urbs, urbis**, f.	city
iaciō, iacere*	I throw		
		adverb	
adjectives		**fortiter**	bravely
cārus, -a, -um	dear		
fortis, forte	brave	*preposition*	
omnis, omne	all	**ā/ab** + abl.	from

* notice that these verbs are of the **capiō** class (mixed conjugation)

What is (a) a *pugnacious* man, (b) a *navigational* aid, (c) an *urban* council, (d) *fraternal* love, (e) *regal* splendour, (f) *omnipotent* God? (What do you suppose the Latin adjective **potēns** means?) From what Latin words are the English words in italics derived?

Flavius' story: The siege of Troy

Agamemnōn, rēx Mycēnārum, omnēs prīncipēs Graecōrum convocat; iubet eōs bellum in Trōiānōs parāre. frāter eius, Menelāus, adest; Achillēs, hērōum fortissimus, venit ā Thessaliā; adest Ulixēs ab Ithacā cum comitibus, et multī aliī. magnum
5 exercitum parant et multās nāvēs. ad urbem Trōiam nāvigant et Trōiānōs oppugnant.

Mycēnārum of Mycenae
Graecōrum of the Greeks
bellum war; **eius** his
hērōum fortissimus the bravest of the heroes
Ulixēs = Odysseus; **exercitum** army

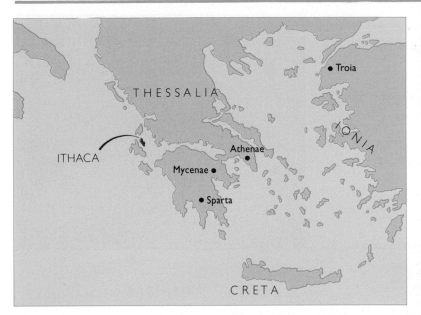

Map of Greece

The Lion Gate at Mycenae

sed Trōiānī urbem fortiter dēfendunt. decem annōs Graecī
urbem obsident sed eam capere nōn possunt. tandem
Agamemnōn et Achillēs in rixam cadunt. Achillēs īrātus est; nōn
10 diūtius pugnat sed prope navēs manet ōtiōsus. Trōiānī iam
Graecōs vincunt et pellunt ad nāvēs.

Agamemnōn amīcōs ad Achillem mittit quī eum iubent ad
pugnam redīre. illī 'ō Achillēs,' inquiunt, 'Trōiānī nōs vincunt et
pellunt ad nāvēs. in magnō perīculō sumus. tū dēbēs ad pugnam
15 redīre et comitēs dēfendere.' sed ille amīcōs nōn audit neque ab
īrā dēsistit.

mox Trōiānī nāvēs oppugnant et incendunt. Patroclus, amīcus
cārus, ad Achillem accēdit et 'Trōiānī iam nāvēs incendunt,'
inquit. 'dēbēs ab īrā dēsistere et amīcōs iuvāre. sī tū pugnāre nōn
20 vīs, dēbēs mē cum comitibus tuīs in pugnam mittere.' itaque
Achillēs invītus Patroclum in pugnam mittit. ille arma Achillis
induit et comitēs in pugnam dūcit.

Trōiānī, ubi arma Achillis vident, territī sunt et ad urbem
fugiunt. Patroclus in eōs currit et multōs occīdit. sed Hector,
25 fortissimus Trōiānōrum, resistit et Patroclum in pugnam vocat.
hastam iacit et Patroclum interficit.

decem annōs for ten years
obsident besiege
possunt can, are able to
rixam quarrel
nōn diūtius no longer; ōtiōsus idle
pellunt drive; quī who
inquiunt (they) say; nōs (acc.) us
vincunt are conquering
perīculō danger
dēsistit ceases
incendunt set fire to

sī if; nōn vīs are not willing

invītus unwilling(ly), reluctant(ly)
arma Achillis the arms of Achilles
induit puts on; territī terrified

fortissimus Trōiānōrum the bravest
    of the Trojans
hastam spear; interficit kills

Word-building

eō = I go; dūcō = I lead.

What do the following verbs mean:

in-eō, ad-eō, ab-eō, red-eō?
in-dūcō, ad-dūcō, ab-dūcō, re-dūcō?

45

Respondē Latīnē

1 cūr Agamemnōn amīcōs ad Achillem
mittit?
2 quid dīcunt amīcī?
3 cūr Achillēs Patroclum in pugnam mittit?
4 cūr fugiunt Trōiānī ad urbem?

Agamemnon and Achilles

Fābella: lūdus Flāviī

Flāviī of Flavius

Personae: **Flāvius** (*magister*); **Quīntus, Decimus, Gāius** (*puerī*);
Horātia, Iūlia (*puellae*)

Flāvius puerōs in lūdō exspectat. intrant puerī et magistrum
salūtant.

exspectat is waiting for

5 **puerī**: salvē, magister.

salvē greetings!

Flāvius: salvēte, puerī. intrāte celeriter et sedēte.

intrāte come in!; sedēte sit!

omnēs puerī sedent et tacent.

tacent are silent

Flāvius: hodiē, puerī, dēbētis dīligenter labōrāre et litterās bene
scrībere.

10 *omnēs puellae labōrant, sed Gāius nōn labōrat; Iūliam spectat.*

Gāius: (*susurrat*) Iūlia, vīsne domum hodiē mēcum venīre?

susurrat whispers

Iūlia: (*susurrat*) tacē, Gāī. Flāvius nōs spectat.

vīsne? won't you?

Flāvius: quid facis, Gāī? cūr nōn labōrās?

tacē be quiet!

Gāius: ego, magister? ego dīligenter labōrō et litterās bene

bene well

15 scrībō.

Flāvius: vēnī hūc, Gāī; tuam tabulam spectāre cupiō.

vēnī hūc come here!

Gāius ad Flāvium adit.

Gāius: ecce, magister. litterās bene scrībō.

Flāvius: litterās nōn bene scrībis, Gāī. ignāvus es.

ignāvus lazy

20 *Gāius ad sellam redit et paulīsper labōrat. Horātia omnēs*
litterās iam scrīpsit et pictūrās in tabulā scrībit. Flāvius ad
eam accēdit et tabulam spectat.

sellam his seat
paulīsper for a little
scrīpsit has written

Flāvius: Horātia, quid facis?

Horātia: litterās scrībō, magister. ecce!

25 **Flāvius**: nōn litterās scrībis sed pictūrās. ignāva es. litterās
iterum scrībe.

scrībe write!

Quīntus, quī omnēs litterās iam scrīpsit, cessat; subitō
Scintillam videt per fenestram; illa Argum dūcit per viam.

cessat is idling
fenestram window

Quīntus: (*susurrat*) Arge, bone canis, venī hūc.

30   *Argus Quīntum audit; ad fenestram currit et lātrat. Flāvius ad*   **lātrat** barks
      fenestram festīnat.

Flāvius: abī, male canis. quid facis? abī statim.   **abī** go away!

      Argus per fenestram salit et Quīntum salūtat; deinde per   **salit** jumps
      lūdum currit et Horātiam quaerit. omnēs puerī surgunt et   **quaerit** looks for
35   *Argum petunt. Flāvius dēspērat.*   **petunt** chase; **dēspērat** despairs

Flāvius: abīte, puerī. vōs dīmittō. tū, Quīnte, dūc illum canem   **vōs** (acc.) you; **dūc** lead! take!
      ē lūdō.

HOMER AND THE ILIAD – I

Besides reading, writing and arithmetic, children would learn
both from their parents and from their teachers the stories of
Greece and Rome which were part of the common culture of the
ancient world. The most powerful of these focused on the sack of
Troy by the Greeks; and this cycle of stories was linked to Rome,
since the Romans believed that their ancestors were Trojans who
had escaped when Troy was taken.

Homer

This story had been told in Greek by the first and some would
say the greatest poet of Western literature. He probably lived
before 700 BC and his name was Homer. We know almost nothing
about him. He came from Ionia in what is now western Turkey,
and according to tradition he was blind. He may have composed
both the *Iliad* and the *Odyssey*, the great poems which have come
down to us under his name, but even that is uncertain. The *Iliad*
is the tragic story of the terrible events which led up to the sack
of Troy, a city in north-west Turkey, by the Greeks. The *Odyssey*
tells of Odysseus' return from Troy to Greece and his recovery of
his kingdom, and the adventures and dangers he met in the
process.

In this chapter the schoolmaster tells the story of the *Iliad*. We
now summarize the events which come before the action of
Homer's poem.

The gods held a great wedding feast to celebrate the marriage
of Peleus and Thetis. The goddess Eris (Strife), however, had not
been invited. Furious at this insult, she stormed into the hall
where the feast was taking place and flung down a golden apple.
Inscribed upon this were the words 'For the most beautiful'.

As Eris had planned, the apple was going to prove the cause
of terrible troubles. The obvious candidates for the title of most
beautiful goddess were Juno, Minerva and Venus.
Understandably, none of the gods was prepared to make the
decision between them. The judge would have to face the anger
of the two losers, whichever of the three won! Jupiter therefore
decided that a mortal must settle the matter, and his choice fell on

the Trojan prince Paris. He was extremely good-looking and seemed likely to be highly experienced in such matters.

So the goddesses flew to Mount Ida near Troy where Paris was tending his flocks. After he had overcome his astonishment and realized what was expected of him, all three of them tried to bribe him to give them the apple. Juno offered him a vast kingdom, Minerva promised him military glory, and Venus said that she would give him the most beautiful woman in the world. This was Helen, the wife of Menelaus, king of Sparta in Greece. Venus' offer seemed the most attractive to Paris and he presented the apple to her.

Paris now went to stay with Menelaus in Sparta. Here he and Helen fell in love with each other and they ran off back to Troy. Menelaus joined with his brother Agamemnon, king of Mycenae, to lead a huge expedition of Greeks against Troy in order to bring the faithless wife home again. Helen's face 'launched a thousand ships'.

But the war that took place around the walls of Troy did not go well for the Greeks. Homer's *Iliad* begins by telling of the disastrous quarrel which arose when King Agamemnon took from Achilles, the greatest of the Greek warriors, a slave girl who had been given to Achilles by the army. This was a devastating blow, not only to the emotions of Achilles, who was very fond of the girl, but far more importantly to his honour. Horace's schoolmaster relates to his pupils the dreadful results of Agamemnon's foolish insult to Achilles.

If you had been in Paris' position, which choice would you have made?

Troy

puerī prope iānuam lūdī manent; magister dīcit: 'intrāte, puerī, et sedēte!'

Quīntus sērō advenit; magister dīcit: 'cūr sērō advenīs, Quīnte? intrā celeriter et sedē.'

puerī sedent sed nōn labōrant. magister dīcit: 'nōlīte lūdere, puerī, sed audīte.'

magister ad Horātiam accēdit et dīcit: 'Horātia, nōlī pictūrās in tabulā scrībere.'

Note that the cartoons introduce a new part of the verb, which is used to give commands.

Vocabulary 8

verbs		*nouns*		*adverbs*	
possum, posse	I can, I am able	**hasta, -ae**, f.	spear	**bene**	well
exspectō, -āre	I wait for	**porta, -ae**, f.	gate	**hīc**	here
servō, -āre	I save	**mūrus, -ī**, m.	wall	**hūc**	(to) here, hither
timeō, -ēre	I fear, I am afraid	**māter, mātris**, f.	mother		
reddō, -ere	I return, give back	**mors, mortis**, f.	death	*conjunction*	
relinquō, -ere	I leave behind			**-que**	and
vertō, -ere	I turn	*adjectives*			
coniciō, -ere	I hurl	**mortuus, -a, -um**	dead		
		sōlus, -a, -um	alone		
prepositions		**territus, -a, -um**	terrified		
circum + acc.	round	**incolumis, incolume**	safe, unharmed		
ē/ex + abl.	out of, from				

The death of Hector

Achillēs, ubi Patroclus mortuus est, eum diū lūget; Hectorem   **lūget** mourns
vindicāre cupit. redit ad pugnam et comitēs in Trōiānōs dūcit. illī,   **vindicāre** take vengeance on
ubi Achillem vident, territī sunt; in urbem fugiunt. Hector sōlus
extrā mūrōs manet.   **extrā mūrōs** outside the walls

5   pater Priamus, rēx Trōiae, et māter Hecuba eum vident ē
mūrīs; fīlium vocant; Priamus clāmat: 'Hector, nōlī Achillem in
pugnam vocāre; nōn potes eum vincere. urbem intrā; festīnā.'
māter clāmat: 'fīlī cāre, nōlī extrā mūrōs manēre; nōlī mortem
obīre; māter tua misera tē ōrat.'   **obīre** go to meet
10   sed Hector eōs nōn audit; urbem intrāre nōn vult. Trōiānōs   **ōrat** beseeches, begs
vocat et 'portās claudite, Trōiānī,' inquit; 'festīnāte. ego sōlus   **nōn vult** refuses; **claudite** close!
maneō extrā mūrōs et Achillem ad pugnam vocō.'
     Trōiānī invītī portās claudunt. Hector sōlus Achillem   **invītī** unwilling(ly)
exspectat. ille propius accēdit. tum Hector subitō timet. tergum   **propius** nearer; **tergum** back
15 vertit et fugit.
     Achillēs celeriter currit sed eum capere nōn potest. ter circum   **ter** three times
mūrōs fugit Hector, sed tandem resistit; sē vertit et Achillem in   **sē vertit** he turns round

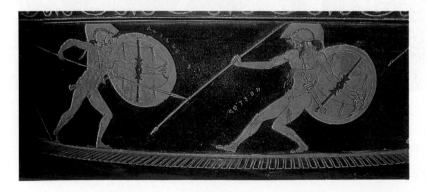

Achilles and Hector

pugnam vocat. ille prōcēdit et hastam in Hectorem conicit. sed
Hector hastam vītat. deinde Hector hastam conicit et Achillis
20 parmam percutit. sed Achillēs incolumis est; nam parma eum
servat.

    deinde Achillēs hastam summā vī conicit; volat hasta per
auram et Hectorem trānsfīgit. ille ad terram cadit mortuus.

    accurrit Achillēs et dīrum facinus facit. Hectorem mortuum
25 ad currum alligat et circum mūrōs trahit. pater et māter ē mūrīs
spectant. Hecuba clāmat: 'ō Achillēs,' inquit, 'tandem ab īrā
dēsiste; fīlium nōbīs redde.' sed Achillēs eam nōn audit;
Hectorem ad nāvēs trahit et eum relinquit in terrā iacentem.

vītat avoids
Achillis parmam Achilles' shield
percutit strikes
summā vī with all his might
volat flies
auram air; **trānsfīgit** pierces
dīrum facinus (acc.) a terrible deed
currum chariot; **alligat** ties
trahit drags; **dēsiste** cease from!
nōbīs to us; **iacentem** lying

Achilles dragging Hector's body
around the walls of Troy

In this story you find the sentences:

    ter circum mūrōs fugit Hector = three times round the walls
        flees Hector.
    volat hasta per auram = through the air flies the spear.
    accurrit Achillēs = up runs Achilles.

In these sentences the subject follows the verb; this word order
can be used quite freely in Latin, since the case ending shows
which word is subject. This word order places more emphasis on
the verb without changing the sense.

Word-building

Every chapter from now on contains an exercise showing how
you can build up your Latin vocabulary by seeing how words you
have not met are formed from those you have learnt, e.g.

    cēn-a = dinner; **cēn-ō** = I dine.

What do the following pairs of words mean?

nouns	verbs
pugn-a	pugn-ō
vōx, vōc-is	voc-ō
rēx, rēg-is	reg-ō
laus, laud-is	laud-ō
dux, duc-is	dūc-ō
labor, labōr-is	labōr-ō

The ransom of Hector

Without translating, answer the questions below

diū māter fīlium mortuum lūget; diū lūget Andromachē uxor
Hectoris; diū lūget Priamus. tandem, ubi nox venit, Priamus ex
urbe exit et sōlus ad Graecōrum nāvēs prōcēdit. deus Mercurius
eum dūcit per vigilēs Graecōrum. tandem ad Achillis
5 tabernāculum advenit; intrat et Achillem salūtat; ad terram
prōcumbit et 'ō Achillēs, tē ōrō,' inquit; 'tandem ab īrā dēsiste et
fīlium mortuum ad mātrem miseram remitte.'

   Achillēs, ubi Priamum videt, attonitus est. misericordiā
commōtus est; Priamum ē terrā tollit. fīlium mortuum reddit et
10 patrem ad urbem Trōiam incolumem remittit.
   unharmed

luget mourns; **uxor** wife

nox night

Graecōrum of the Greeks; **deus** god

vigilēs watchmen, guards

Achillis tabernāculum Achilles' tent

prōcumbit he bows down

ōrō I beg

misericordiā by pity

commōtus est he is moved

tollit raises, lifts up

1 What does Priam do, when night comes? [3]
2 How does he find his way through the Greek guards? [2]
3 What does he do when he enters Achilles' tent? [4]
4 How does Achilles react to Priam's words? [2]
5 Does Achilles' behaviour here change our view
   of his character? [5]

THE ILIAD – 2

In this chapter, we have briefly told the end of the story of the
Iliad. We described how Achilles, although he has now taken
revenge on Hector for killing his friend Patroclus, nevertheless
pushes his hatred beyond his enemy's death. He drags Hector's
corpse round Patroclus' tomb again and again in his wild anger
and grief.

   It was considered a terrible thing in the Greek world to leave
a man unburied, since it meant that his spirit could not find rest
in the next life. Most of the gods disapprove of Achilles'
treatment of Hector's corpse, and Apollo protects it, making sure
that it does not become damaged in any way.

   Jupiter now decides that Achilles must give Hector's body
back to his father Priam. He sends Iris, goddess of the rainbow,
to tell Priam to go to the Greek camp at night and to ask Achilles
to grant him his request. He also sends Thetis, the mother of

Achilles, to see her son and to make sure that he does what he's told.

Priam loads a wagon with a fabulous ransom and sets off for the Greek camp with a single charioteer. As they approach the enemy lines, the god Mercury meets them in disguise and leads them to Achilles' hut. Miraculously they are unnoticed by any of the Greeks. Achilles gazes in amazement as the old man enters, kneels before him and takes hold of the fatal hands which have killed so many of his children.

Priam begs him to accept the ransom and return Hector's corpse, making him imagine the feelings of an old father who has lost his son. The two men, one so young and the other so very old, weep together. Priam remembers Hector and Achilles thinks of his own father Peleus at home in Greece, destined never to see his son again. For Achilles had been given the choice between a short life with immortal fame and a long but obscure existence. He had chosen the former.

The ransom of Hector

As the two enemies weep, the anger of Achilles disappears and he agrees to Priam's request. They eat together and later that night Priam leaves the Greek camp, again under the protection of Mercury. He returns to the city with his son's body on the wagon which had carried the ransom on the way out. The Trojans will be given the opportunity to pay full funeral rites to Hector back at Troy, during a truce guaranteed by Achilles.

Two dreadful events hang over the end of the *Iliad*. One of them is the death of Achilles. He will be mortally wounded by an arrow in his heel, the only part of his body where a weapon can penetrate. The other is the fall of Troy which cannot be avoided now that Hector is dead. So Achilles and Priam will soon join Patroclus and Hector and the countless other victims of the Trojan War in the Underworld.

Explain the causes of Achilles' anger against first the Greeks and then the Trojans.

How do the events described above bring the Iliad *to a satisfactory conclusion?*

puer puellae cēnam rapit.

(handwritten: of the girl, snatches)

puella capsulam (*satchel*) puerī rapit.

(handwritten: of the boy)

māter puellārum pictūrās spectat.

(handwritten: of the girls)

māter tabulās puerōrum spectat.

(handwritten: of the boys)

fīlius patris agrum init.

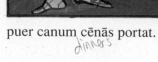

puer canum cēnās portat.

(handwritten: dinners)

The captions introduce the genitive case = 'of'.

Vocabulary 9

Some 3rd declension adjectives have the same form for masculine, feminine and neuter in the nominative singular; these are listed with the nominative and genitive, e.g. **ingēns, ingentis**

verbs

gaudeō, -ēre	I rejoice
habeō, -ēre	I have
moneō, -ēre	I warn, advise
taceō, -ēre	I am silent
bibō, -ere	I drink
cōnscendō, -ere	I board (a ship)
conveniō, -īre	I come together, meet
accipiō, -ere	I receive

nouns

īnsula, -ae, f.	island
equus, equī, m.	horse
vir, virī, m.	man
labor, labōris, m.	work, hardship, suffering
nox, noctis, f.	night
uxor, uxōris, f.	wife

adjectives

novus, -a, -um	new
parvus, -a, -um	small
paucī, -ae, -a	few
tacitus, -a, -um	silent
tōtus, -a, -um	whole
ingēns, ingentis	huge

adverb

sīc	thus

preposition

inter + acc.	among, between

The fall of Troy

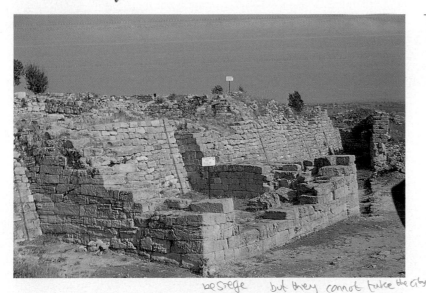

The ruined walls of Troy

decem annōs Graecī Trōiānōs obsident sed urbem capere nōn
possunt. tandem Agamemnōn, rēx Graecōrum, dēspērat; omnēs
prīncipēs convenīre iubet et 'decem annōs iam Trōiam
obsidēmus,' inquit; 'saepe Trōiānōs in pugnā vincimus sed urbem
5 capere nōn possumus. ego dēspērō. quid facere dēbēmus?
domumne redīre dēbēmus? quid vōs monētis?'

decem annōs for ten years
obsident besiege; **dēspērat** despairs

cēterī prīncipēs tacent, sed Ulixēs 'ego nōn dēspērō,' inquit;
'cōnsilium novum habeō. audīte mē.'

omnēs prīncipēs cōnsilium Ulixis attentē audiunt; cōnsilium
10 laetī accipiunt. equum ligneum faciunt, ingentem; multōs virōs
fortēs in equum immittunt. illī in equum ascendunt et in ventre
equī sē cēlant. cēterī nāvēs cōnscendunt et nāvigant ad īnsulam
vīcīnam.

prīmā lūce Trōiānī nāvēs Graecōrum vident abeuntēs; gaudent
15 quod Graecī nōn adsunt, gaudent quod pugnae tandem cōnfectae
sunt. ē portīs urbis currunt ad ōram dēsertam; equum ingentem
spectant in ōrā stantem. aliī 'equum dēbēmus in urbem dūcere,'
inquiunt. aliī 'equō nōlite crēdere,' inquiunt; 'timēmus Graecōrum
dōna. fortasse Graecī in eō cēlātī sunt.' tandem cōnstituunt eum
20 in urbem dūcere. omnēs laetī eum per portās trahunt et in arce
pōnunt. deinde epulās faciunt et multum vīnum bibunt.

nox adest. dormiunt Trōiānī. Graecī quī in īnsulā sunt nāvēs
cōnscendunt et celeriter ad urbem Trōiam redeunt. eī, quī in equō
cēlātī sunt, tacitī exeunt et festīnant ad portās.

25 vigilēs Trōiānōrum dormiunt; ēbriī sunt. Graecī eōs occīdunt;
portās celeriter aperiunt et comitēs accipiunt. omnēs in viās urbis
currunt. paucī Trōiānōrum resistunt. mox Graecī tōtam urbem
capiunt. tandem rēgiam Priamī oppugnant; Priamum et fīliōs eius
occīdunt. paucī ēvādunt. sīc Graecī tandem Trōiam capiunt et
30 urbem dēlent.

cōnsilium plan

ligneum wooden
in ventre in the belly
sē cēlant hide themselves
vīcīnam neighbouring
prīmā lūce at first light
abeuntēs going away
cōnfectae finished; ōram shore
stantem standing
equō … crēdere trust the horse
dōna (acc. pl.) gifts
fortasse perhaps; cēlātī hidden
in arce in the citadel
epulās a feast; vīnum wine
quī who; eī those (men)

vigilēs watchmen; ēbriī drunk
aperiunt open

rēgiam palace
ēvādunt escape
dēlent destroy

The Trojan horse

Respondē Latīnē

1 ubi nox venit, quid faciunt Graecī?
2 quid faciunt Graecī quī in equō sunt?
3 cūr nōn resistunt Trōiānōrum vigilēs?

Word-building

What do the following pairs of nouns mean?

fīlius	fīlia
amīcus	amīca
dominus (= *master*)	domina
servus (= *slave*)	serva
rēx, rēg-is	rēgīna

The
death
of Priam

Aenēās ex urbe Trōiā fugit

Read the following passage and without translating answer the questions below

Trōiānōrum paucī ēvādunt; urbem ardentem relinquunt et fugiunt
in montēs. inter eōs est Aenēās, prīnceps Trōiānus; ille patrem et
uxorem et parvum fīlium ē flammīs ēripit et ad montēs dūcit.
mox aliī ad montēs conveniunt. omnēs dēspērant, sed Aenēās
'Trōia incēnsa est,' inquit, 'sed nōs Trōiānī supersumus. venīte
mēcum. novam Trōiam in aliā terrā condere dēbēmus.'

illī Aenēam laetī audiunt. montēs relinquunt et ad ōram
dēscendunt; nāvēs cōnscendunt et mox ab urbe Trōiā in terrās
ignōtās nāvigant. diū in undīs errant et multōs labōrēs subeunt.
tandem in Italiam veniunt et urbem condunt.

ēvādunt escape; **ardentem** burning
montēs mountains
ēripit rescues

incēnsa burnt
supersumus we survive
mēcum with me; **condere** found
ōram shore
ignōtās unknown; **undīs** waves
errant wander; **subeunt** undergo

1 Whom does Aeneas rescue from Troy and where does he take them? [4]
2 How does Aeneas encourage the surviving Trojans? [4]
3 Where do they sail to and how do they fare on the voyage? [4]

VIRGIL AND THE AENEID

Horace's friend Publius Vergilius Maro, known in English as Virgil, was born in 70 BC and so was five years older than Horace. He was brought up on his father's farm at Mantua in North Italy, and completed his education in Rome and Naples. He belonged to a group of poets who celebrated in their work the first Roman emperor Augustus. Horace, who described Virgil as 'half of my soul', was also one of the group.

Virgil and two Muses

Virgil's greatest poem was the *Aeneid*. It was in twelve books, begun in 29 BC and still unfinished at his death in 19 BC. Its central figure is Aeneas, the son of Venus and the Trojan Anchises. The story tells how he flees from the smoking ruins of Troy and travels to Italy where Destiny plans that he should found the Roman race.

We now describe the events of that dreadful night in more detail than was possible in the Latin.

On the night when their city fell the Trojans held joyful celebrations, wrongly believing that the Greeks had given up their siege and departed. The whole of Troy was buried in slumber and wine. The ghost of Hector appeared to Aeneas as he lay sleeping. Aeneas was horribly shocked by his appearance, for he was black with the dust through which Achilles had dragged him when he killed him. But Hector paid no attention to Aeneas' reaction, and told him that Troy was now in the enemy's hands. He ordered him to rescue the Trojan gods from the burning city and to sail away to found a new Troy in some other country.

Aeneas was now thoroughly awakened by the noise of the fighting, and climbing to the top of his house he saw the flames which were sweeping through the city. Hector's instructions vanished from his mind and he ran into the streets where he fought with tremendous courage, killing many Greeks. A dreadful sight met his eyes as he reached the royal palace. He saw Achilles' son slaughter King Priam on the step of the altar itself. Aeneas' anger burned fiercely as he sought vengeance for the destruction of Troy.

But now his mother Venus appeared to him and reminded him that his duty was to his family. He must try, she said, to bring them to safety. Aeneas realized that she was right. There was no longer anything he could do for Troy. He rushed back to his house, gathered together his followers and made his way from the city. He bore on his shoulders his father, who carried the little statues of the household gods, and he held his son by the hand. His wife followed them as they set out on this terrifying journey.

Suddenly Aeneas was aware that his wife was no longer behind him. Desperately he ran back into the city, now eerily still, calling her name again and again, but there was no answer. Finally her ghost appeared to him. She told him that she was dead. He must set out for the new land which awaited him. Three times Aeneas attempted to fling his arms around his wife. Three times his wife's ghost dissolved in his embrace like the light winds.

He returned sadly to his companions who were safely hidden in a hollow valley in the mountains by Troy. A dangerous and uncertain future awaited them.

Aeneas carrying his father from Troy

Imagine that you are a Greek hidden in the wooden horse. Describe what happens to you and what you do.

Virgil often describes Aeneas as pius *or 'dutiful'. How well do you think that this description suits him in the way he leaves Troy?*

Trōiānī ad lītus Siciliae nāvigant.
to the shore of

smokes *throwouts*
mōns Aetna fūmum et saxa in caelum prōicit;
Trōiānī in magnō perīculō sunt.
are in great danger

they rest *down from*
dum in lītore quiēscunt, Polyphēmum vident; dē
monte lentē dēscendit.

Polyphēmus in mare prōcēdit et saxa in nāvēs
conicit.
hurls

Vocabulary 10

verbs		nouns		prepositions	
habitō, -āre	I live, dwell	**nauta, -ae**, m.	sailor	**dē** + abl.	down from
ōrō, -āre	I pray, beg	**silva, -ae**, f.	wood	**sub** + abl.	under
quaerō, -ere	I ask, I seek	**unda, -ae**, f.	wave		
quiēscō, -ere	I rest	**caelum, -ī**, n.	sky, heaven		
tollō, -ere	I lift, raise	**perīculum, -ī**, n.	danger		
		saxum, -ī, n.	rock		
adjective		**verbum, -ī**, n.	word		
prīmus, -a, -um	first	**clāmor, clāmōris**, m.	shout		
		homō, hominis, c.	man, human being		
adverbs		**lītus, lītoris**, n.	shore		
prīmum	first	**mare, maris**, n.	sea		
vix	scarcely	**mōns, montis**, m.	mountain		

Polyphēmus

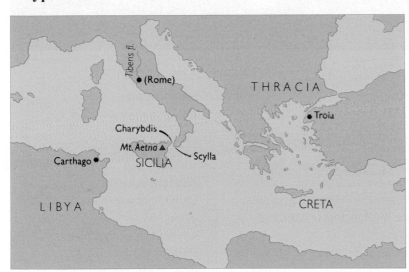

The travels of Aeneas

Aenēās et Trōiānī nāvēs cōnscendunt; ab urbe Trōiā in terrās
ignōtās nāvigant. diū terram quaerunt ubi novam Trōiam condere
possunt; multōs labōrēs, multa perīcula subeunt; saepe dēspērat
Aenēās. tandem cōnstituunt ad Italiam nāvigāre.

5   sed ubi ad Siciliam accēdunt, magnum perīculum vix vītant,
nam saxa vident ubi habitat Scylla, mōnstrum horribile, et
sonitum ingentem audiunt verticis ubi Charybdis undās ēvomit.
pater Anchīsēs magnā vōce clāmat: 'fugite; nāvēs ē perīculō
ēripite; nam in illīs saxīs habitat Scylla.' Aenēās patris verba audit
10 et saxa vītat. sīc vix incolumēs ē perīculō ēvādunt.

    ubi ad Siciliam veniunt, montem Aetnam vident; nāvēs ad
terram dīrigunt et sub noctem ad lītus īnsulae adveniunt. sub

ignōtās unknown; **ubi** where
subeunt undergo; **dēspērat** despairs

vītant avoid
mōnstrum a monster
sonitum sound
verticis of the whirlpool
ēvomit spews out
magnā vōce in a loud voice
ēripite snatch, rescue
dīrigunt steer
sub noctem towards nightfall

Mount Etna

monte in lītore quiēscunt. mōns Aetna per noctem tonat; flammās
et saxa in caelum prōicit. Trōiānī territī sunt et ānxiī diem
15 exspectant.

festīnant nāvēs cōnscendere cum hominem vident, quī ad lītus
currit. Trōiānōs vocat; accurrit ad eōs et 'servāte mē,' inquit, 'vōs
ōrō. ego Graecus sum, comes Ulixis. cēterī fūgērunt. ego sōlus
maneō. fugite, miserī, fugite. Cyclōpēs hīc habitant, gigantēs
20 immānēs, quī hominēs edunt. nōlīte mē Cyclōpibus trādere.
servāte mē, accipite mē in nāvem.'

subitō Trōiānī Polyphēmum vident, gigantem ingentem. ille
ovēs dē monte dūcit. caecus est; lentē dēscendit; in viā saepe
lāpsat. Aenēās territus est. 'currite ad nāvēs,' inquit; 'festīnāte!'
25 Trōiānī comitem Ulixis accipiunt et fugiunt ad nāvēs.

Polyphēmus iam ad lītus advenit et in mare prōcēdit. Trōiānōs
vidēre nōn potest sed audit eōs rēmigantēs. clāmōrem ingentem
tollit. cēterī Cyclōpēs clāmōrem audiunt et currunt dē montibus
ad lītus. saxa ingentia in nāvēs coniciunt; sed Trōiānī iam ē lītore
30 rēmigant. Cyclōpēs eōs contingere nōn possunt.

tonat thunders
prōicit throws up; diem day

cum when; quī who
vōs (acc.) you
fūgērunt have fled
gigantēs immānēs enormous giants
edunt eat
Cyclōpibus to the Cyclopes
trādere to hand over
ovēs sheep; caecus blind
lāpsat slips

rēmigantēs rowing

contingere reach

Word-building

What do the following verbs mean?

currō: incurrō, accurrō (= ad-currō), concurrō, recurrō, dēcurrō
veniō: adveniō, reveniō, conveniō

Fābella: Aeneas escapes from Polyphemus

Persōnae: Aenēās, Nauta prīmus, Nauta alter, Graecus, Polyphēmus

alter second

Trōiānī in lītore Siciliae quiēscunt sub monte Aetnā.

Nauta prīmus: nōn cupiō hīc diū manēre; vidē montem; saxa
flammāsque in caelum prōicit.

prōicit throws up

5 **Nauta alter**: cavē! saxum ingēns dē monte cadit. nōn possumus
hīc dormīre.

cavē! look out!

Nauta prīmus: ecce! aliquis dē monte hūc dēcurrit.

aliquis someone

Nauta alter: eum videō, hominem squālidum et miserum.

squālidum filthy

Nauta prīmus: quis est? Aenēā, cavē! homō squālidus et miser
10 dē monte hūc dēcurrit.

Aenēās surgit hominemque spectat. homō accēdit.

Aenēās: heus! quis es? quid facis? cūr hūc curris?

heus! hey!

Graecus: servāte mē, vōs ōrō. Graecus sum, comes Ulixis.
cēterī fūgērunt. ego sōlus maneō. fugite, miserī,

fūgērunt have fled

15 fugite. gigantēs ingentēs hīc habitant quī hominēs
edunt. servāte mē.

edunt eat

Nauta prīmus: nōlī nūgās nārrāre. nūllī gigantēs sunt nisi in
fābulīs puerīlibus.

nūgās nonsense; **nūllī** no
nisi except

Nauta alter: dī immortālēs! vidēte! ille gigas nōn fābulōsus est.

dī immortālēs immortal gods!

20 **Aenēās**: fugite, amīcī. ad nāvēs currite. et tū, Graece, venī
nōbīscum.

nōbīscum with us

*Trōiānī nāvēs cōnscendunt et ē lītore rēmigant. Polyphēmus ad
mare dēscendit et in undās prōcēdit. subitō cōnsistit et auram
olfacit; ingentem clāmōrem tollit.*

cōnsistit stops

auram olfacit sniffs the air

25 **Polyphēmus**: phī, phae, phō, phum
sanguinem olfaciō Trōiānōrum virum.

sanguinem blood

venīte, Cyclōpēs, festīnāte! dē monte dēcurrite.
Trōiānī adsunt; festīnāte, nisi cēnam crāstinam
perdere cupitis.

nisi unless; **crāstinam** tomorrow's
perdere to lose

30

35

40

*Cyclōpēs conveniunt et ad
lītus dēcurrunt. saxa
ingentia in nāvēs coniciunt
sed Trōiānōs contingere nōn
possunt. Aenēās in puppe
nāvis stat et Cyclōpēs
irrīdet.*

puppe stern

irrīdet mocks

Aenēās: ō stultī Cyclōpēs,
sērō advenītis. vōs nōn
timēmus. aliam cēnam
quaerite. nōn potestis nōs
edere. valēte, caudicēs.

valēte goodbye
caudicēs blockheads

Polyphemus

63

THE AENEID – 2

All nations have their heroes. We know the famous stories of King Arthur and King Alfred, and of George Washington. The Romans had their legend of Aeneas, the Trojan prince who fled from Troy, brought his followers to Italy and founded the Roman nation.

Virgil, the greatest of all Roman poets, describes the adventures of Aeneas in his poem, the *Aeneid*. The first half of this poem tells of the travels of Aeneas as he tries to find his way from Troy to the site of Rome. It owes much to Homer's *Odyssey*, which is about the journey home of the Greek hero Odysseus. The *Odyssey* is centred on Odysseus. His Latin name is Ulixes, and that is how we have referred to him in our Latin story.

The first three words of the *Aeneid* – *arma virumque canō* ('I sing of arms and the man') – not only introduce the story of the warrior Aeneas but inform us of what the poem is to be about. *arma* (arms) brings to mind the *Iliad*. Its subject, as we have seen, is the fighting round the city of Troy, and in it the Trojan prince Aeneas plays a minor but significant role. *virum* (man) calls the *Odyssey* to mind. The first word of that poem is the Greek word for 'man' and it tells not simply of the hero Odysseus' adventures as he travels from the Trojan War back to his island of Ithaca, but also of the way he re-establishes himself as king there.

By making his readers think of Homer right at the outset, Virgil shows astonishing ambition in putting his work on a level with that of his great predecessor. He sets his hero in the same world as Achilles, Hector, Priam and the other noble figures of the Trojan War, and he adds a Homeric dimension to the travels of Aeneas (the first half of the *Aeneid*) by modelling them on the *Odyssey*, and then to the dreadful war that Aeneas is to undergo in Italy (the second half of the poem), which he models on the *Iliad*.

But the differences between Homer and the *Aeneid* are as important as the similarities. Odysseus, for example, is travelling back to his homeland and his wife. Aeneas' home of Troy lies in ruins and he must journey towards a mysterious future and a city and empire of Rome which he will never see. Odysseus loses all of his companions and arrives at Ithaca alone. Aeneas is a leader of a new kind with a social responsibility, and many of his men reach Italy. *Pietās* (sense of duty) – you met the adjective *pius* in the last chapter – is the key to his character. He only briefly forgets his duty to his family, his gods and his men.

The endlessly inventive Odysseus, as you will discover, revels in the challenging dangers which confront him in a hostile world. Aeneas' destiny involves him in labours which he undergoes doggedly. Odysseus loves his wife and manages to part with his mistresses on friendly terms. Aeneas, on the other hand, loses his wife and is soon to embark on a disastrous love affair. Through the way he portrays Aeneas, the ancestor of the Romans and of their first emperor Augustus, Virgil tells us of the Roman sense of their mission which was to make them great. He also makes clear to us the tragic suffering which that mission left in its wake.

But now let us leave Aeneas for a moment and look at some of the adventures of his prototype Odysseus.

Odysseus and the Cyclops

On his travels Odysseus meets with many adventures, but perhaps the most famous of all is his encounter with the Cyclops. The Cyclopes were a race of one-eyed giants, a savage people without laws who lived in caves in the mountains of Sicily. Odysseus and his men had the bad fortune to come to their coast.

Odysseus was always extremely curious. He decided to take twelve of his followers to investigate this strange race. They set out, taking with them some wonderful wine in a goatskin, and they soon came to the cave of the Cyclops, who was out in the pasture at the time, tending his sheep. Odysseus' men gazed at all the cheeses, kids and lambs in the cave, and wanted to take some of these away to their ships and sail off as quickly as possible. Odysseus, however, wished to meet the Cyclops, and rashly insisted on staying. At last the huge Cyclops returned with his flocks and, once inside, he rolled an enormous stone in front of the entrance of the cave. He then noticed his visitors, but he showed no signs of hospitality. On the contrary, he grabbed two of them, tore them limb from limb and wolfed them down.

Odysseus offers the Cyclops wine

Odysseus had to think of a trick to enable his men to escape, since direct force would achieve nothing against a giant of such size. The next day the Cyclops went out with his flocks, taking care to put the stone back in place once he was outside. Odysseus found a huge staff of olive-wood lying on the ground, and he and his men sharpened it at one end and hardened the point in the fire.

The Cyclops returned in the evening, and gobbled down two more of his visitors. But wily Odysseus, pretending to be friendly, offered him some of the wine he had brought from the ship. The Cyclops accepted and quickly became very drunk. He asked Odysseus his name, and the tricky Greek replied that he was called 'Nobody'. The Cyclops promised that he would eat Nobody last, making a gruesome joke, and collapsed in a drunken sleep. Morsels of the flesh he had eaten dribbled from his mouth.

Odysseus and his men now took hold of the huge olive-wood staff and heated the point in the fire till it glowed. Then they plunged it in the Cyclops' single eye. The Cyclops awoke in terrible pain and cried out to the neighbouring Cyclopes to help him. They rushed to his cave and asked him who had hurt him. He answered 'Nobody', so they assumed that nothing was the matter and went away. Odysseus laughed to himself at the success of his plan.

Odysseus blinds the Cyclops

Odysseus solved the difficulty of escaping from the cave by tying his men under the bellies of some large rams. The Cyclops removed the stone at dawn and let out the rams to pasture, stroking their backs to see that no one was on them. Once they were some distance from the cave, Odysseus and his men rushed down to the ships. They took the sheep on board with them, and quickly rowed away. (In Virgil's version of the story, which we have followed in this chapter, one of the Greeks is left behind.)

Odysseus could not resist taunting the Cyclops from the ship, gloating over how he had escaped him. The Cyclops flung a great rock into the sea, creating an enormous swell which drove the ship back towards the land. Only by rowing frantically did the crew manage to avoid being swept onto the shore. Another huge stone hurled by the Cyclops fell short of the ship and the swell carried Odysseus and his men to safety.

Imagine that you are one of Odysseus' companions. Describe your adventures.

What do you think of Odysseus? How good a leader was he?

Odysseus escapes from the Cyclops

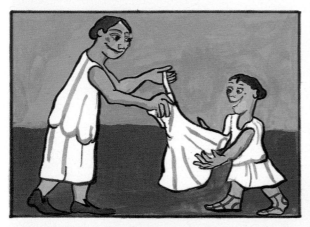

māter Horātiae novam tunicam dat.

pater Quīntō canem dat.

magister puerīs tabulās dat.

puerī parentibus tabulās ostendunt.

Quīntus puellīs flōrēs dat.

The captions introduce the dative case = 'to'.

illae flōrēs eī reddunt.

Vocabulary 11

verbs		*nouns*		*adverb*	
aedificō, -āre	I build	**fāma, -ae,** f.	fame, report, reputation	**semper**	always
errō, -āre	I wander; I err, am wrong	**patria, -ae,** f.	fatherland	*conjunction*	
imperō, -āre + dat.	I order	**rēgīna, -ae,** f.	queen	**dum**	while
stō, stāre	I stand	**somnus, -ī,** m.	sleep		
cognōscō, -ere	I get to know, learn	**ventus, -ī,** m.	wind		
occurrō, -ere + dat.	I meet	**bellum, -ī,** n.	war		
ostendō, -ere	I show	**cōnsilium, -ī,** n.	plan		
succurrō, -ere + dat.	I help	**templum, -ī,** n.	temple		
inveniō, -īre	I find	**vīnum, -ī,** n.	wine		
ferō, ferre	I carry, bear	**arma, -ōrum,** n.pl.	arms, weapons		
		castra, -ōrum, n.pl.	camp		
adjectives		**collis, collis,** m.	hill		
nōtus, -a, -um	known	**hostis, hostis,** c.	enemy		
ignōtus, -a, -um	unknown	**nōmen, nōminis,** n.	name		
		nōmine	by name, called		

The first part of the story of Dido and Aeneas

The meeting of Dido and Aeneas

dum Trōiānī ā Siciliā ad Italiam nāvigant, venit magna tempestās;
Aeolus, rēx ventōrum, omnēs ventōs ēmittit. Trōiānī in magnō
perīculō sunt nec cursum tenēre possunt. tandem ventī eōs ad
terram ignōtam pellunt. Trōiānī ē nāvibus exeunt et in lītore
5 quiēscunt.

postrīdiē Aenēās cōnstituit terram explōrāre. comitibus dīcit:
'vōs prope nāvēs manēte; mihi prōpositum est in terram
prōcēdere.' ūnō cum amīcō collem ascendit et prōspicit. multōs
hominēs videt quī urbem prope lītus aedificant. Aenēās eōs diū
10 spectat. 'ō fortūnātī,' inquit, 'vōs urbem iam aedificātis; nōs
semper in undīs errāmus.' tandem collem dēscendit; urbem intrat
et accēdit ad magnum templum.

in templī mūrīs multae pictūrae sunt; Aenēās pictūrās spectat;
attonitus est; nam pictūrae bellum Trōiānum dēscrībunt. amīcum
15 vocat et 'ecce, amīce,' inquit, 'in hāc pictūrā Priamum vidēre potes
et Achillem. hīc est Agamemnōn. ecce, hīc Achillēs Hectorem
mortuum circum mūrōs urbis trahit. nōlī timēre. Trōiānōrum
labōrēs omnibus nōtī sunt.'

dum templum spectat, ecce, rēgīna, nōmine Dīdō, accēdit
20 multīs cum prīncipibus. Aenēās currit ad eam et 'ō rēgīna,' inquit,
'succurre nōbīs. Trōiānī sumus quī ad Italiam nāvigāmus.
tempestās nōs ad tuam terram pepulit.'

Dīdō Aenēam spectat admīrātiōne plēna; deinde 'fāma
Trōiānōrum,' inquit, 'omnibus nōta est. nōlīte timēre. ego vōbīs
25 laeta succurrō.' sīc eōs benignē accipit et ad rēgiam dūcit. deinde
omnēs prīncipēs Carthāginis et omnēs Trōiānōs ad epulās vocat.

ubi cēna cōnfecta est, Dīdō 'age,' inquit, 'Aenēā, nārrā nōbīs
Trōiae cāsum et omnēs labōrēs Trōiānōrum.' omnēs tacitī sedent et
Aenēam spectant. ille respondet: 'īnfandum, rēgīna, mē iubēs
30 renovāre dolōrem. sed sī cupis cognōscere, audī Trōiae suprēmōs
labōrēs.'

tempestās a storm	
cursum tenēre hold their course	
pellunt drive	
mihi prōpositum est it is my intention	
prōspicit looks out	
fortūnātī lucky	
dēscrībunt portray	
ecce look!; **hāc** this	
trahit drags	
pepulit has driven	
admīrātiōne plēna full of amazement	
benignē kindly; **rēgiam** palace	
epulās feast	
age come on!	
cāsum the fall	
īnfandum ... dolōrem unspeakable grief; **renovāre** to renew; **sī** if	
suprēmōs the last	

Respondē Latīnē

1 dum Aenēās templum spectat, quis ad templum accēdit?
2 quōmodo Dīdō Aenēam accipit?
3 ubi cēna cōnfecta est, quid dīcit Dīdō?

Word-building

What do the following verbs mean?

mittō: immittō, remittō, ēmittō, dīmittō
pōnō: compōnō, dēpōnō, expōnō, impōnō, prōpōnō
cadō: dēcidō, incidō
cēdō: accēdō, discēdō, prōcēdō, recēdō

Fighting round Troy

Aeneas tells of the fall of Troy

Translate the first three paragraphs and answer the questions
below on the fourth paragraph without translating

decem annōs Graecī Trōiam obsident, sed Trōiānī urbem fortiter
dēfendimus. Graecī urbem capere nōn possunt. tandem nāvēs
cōnscendunt et nāvigant in apertum mare. vidēmus eōs abeuntēs
et laetī ex urbe currimus; gaudēmus quod bellum cōnfectum est.
5 festīnāmus ad castra Graecōrum; castra dēserta sunt, sed in lītore
stat ingēns equus. cōnstituimus equum in urbem trahere. deinde
epulās facimus et multum vīnum bibimus.

    nox est. dum dormiō, in somnō Hector mortuus mihi appāret.
ille 'fuge, Aenēā,' inquit; 'hostēs habent mūrōs. Trōia corruit. nōn
10 potes patriam servāre. fuge, et novam Trōiam in aliā terrā conde.'
sīc dīcit Trōiaeque sacra mihi trādit.

    ubi Hectorem audiō, somnum excutiō. ad tēctum ascendō et
urbem ardentem videō. arma capiō et in viās currō. multīs
comitibus occurrō quī in viīs errant. eīs dīcō: 'venīte mēcum et
15 Graecōs oppugnāte.' sed Graecīs resistere nōn diū possumus. mox
tōta urbs ardet.

    subitō patris imāgō in animum mihi venit. domum recurrō.
pater et fīlius et uxor mē exspectant territī. iubeō eōs urbem
mēcum relinquere. patrem in umerīs ferō; parvī fīliī manum
20 teneō; uxōrem iubeō pōne festīnāre. per hostēs, per flammās ad
portās currimus. tandem, ubi ad collēs advenīmus, cōnsistimus.
respiciō, sed uxōrem vidēre nōn possum. in urbem recurrō. diū
uxōrem quaerō, sed frūstrā. tandem ad patrem et fīlium recurrō.

obsident besiege

apertum open; **abeuntēs** going away
cōnfectum finished

epulās feast
mihi to me; **appāret** appears
corruit is collapsing
conde found!
sacra the sacred emblems
excutiō I shake off; **tēctum** roof
ardentem burning

imāgō the thought

in umerīs on my shoulders
manum hand; **teneō** I hold
pōne behind
respiciō I look back
frūstrā in vain

cum eīs multī Trōiānī iam adsunt, quī ex urbe ēvāsērunt. postrīdiē
25 eōs ad lītus dūcō. nāvēs invenīmus; celeriter nāvēs cōnscendimus
et in terrās ignōtās nāvigāmus.

ēvāsērunt have escaped

1 What makes Aeneas run home? [2]
2 Describe the order in which Aeneas and his family
  leave home. [3]
3 What makes him return to Troy? [2]
4 What does he find when he gets back to his father? [3]

DIDO, QUEEN OF CARTHAGE

Dido was the sister of Pygmalion, the cruel king of Tyre in
Phoenicia. She had fallen deeply in love with Sychaeus, a wealthy
landowner, and was very happily married to him. But, tragically,
Pygmalion wanted to lay his hands on his brother-in-law's riches.
In an act of hideous impiety, he killed him as he was praying at
the altar of his household gods, spattering their images with his
blood.

He lulled the wretched Dido's suspicions about the disap-
pearance of her husband by telling her that he was on his travels
and would certainly return. However, one night the ghost of the
still unburied Sychaeus appeared to Dido in a dream, wondrously
pale. He bared his cruel wounds and told Dido what had
happened. He urged her to escape and explained to her where she
could find a vast cache of treasure buried in the earth.

Now came Dido's finest hour. She gathered together a large
number of dissidents who hated or feared the tyrannical
Pygmalion, and they seized a fleet of ships which lay ready to sail
in the harbour. Loading these with Sychaeus' gold and silver, they
set off over the sea. *dux factī erat fēmina*: it was a woman who led
the enterprise.

Arriving in North Africa, Dido bought from the local
chieftains as much land as she could surround with the hide of a
bull. She cut up the bull's hide into a huge length of thread and
thus gained a large kingdom. The resentment of the African
chieftains at this was further inflamed when she rejected the
offers of marriage made by a number of them.

The supremely charismatic Dido now embarked energetically
on the building of a new city, Carthage. Aeneas gazes with
astonishment as he sees the line of walls being laid out and the
enormous stones for the citadel being rolled along. '*ō fortūnātī,
quōrum iam moenia surgunt*' (*quōrum moenia* = whose walls), he
says enviously as he looks up at them. Vast public buildings,
including a great theatre, are being erected. Most wonderful of all
is the temple of Juno where Aeneas sees the pictures of episodes

CHAPTER 11

Aeneas looks down on the building of Carthage

from the Trojan War and feels that the people who dwell here must be sympathetic to the Trojans' suffering.

Dido is on her way to this temple and, as she and Aeneas are about to meet, we are bound to remember how much they have in common. They have both lost their partners in marriage. Both of them, warned by a ghost in a dream, have fled from a city where there is no future for them. Both have shown outstanding courage and leadership. Aeneas' destiny is to found a new city. Dido is already founding one. It seems inevitable that they will be attracted to each other.

Do you feel that, if two such strong personalities, so similar in so many ways, fall in love with each other, they are likely to have a successful and lasting relationship?

And if Aeneas does fall in love with Dido and stays in Carthage to help her with the building of her city, will he betray his pietās, *his essential characteristic? Will his duty to his mission to found the Roman race allow him to stay with Dido?*

And if Dido gives way to love for Aeneas, can she have a relationship with him without betraying the memory of the dead husband whom she had loved so deeply?

Dīdō gladium capit pectusque trānsfīgit.

Vocabulary 12

verbs		*adjectives*	
amō, -āre	I love	**commōtus, -a, -um**	moved
dēspērō, -āre	I despair	**tantus, -a, -um**	so great
placeō, -ēre + dat.	I please	**trīstis, trīste**	sad
mihi placet	it pleases me, I decide	**fēlīx, fēlīcis**	lucky, happy
petō, -ere	I seek, pursue, make for	**īnfēlīx, īnfēlīcis**	unlucky, ill-starred
perficiō, -ere	I carry out		

nouns		*adverbs*		*prepositions*	
animus, -ī, m.	mind	**etiam**	even, also	**ante** + acc.	before
deus, deī, m.	god	**ibi**	there	**post** + acc.	after
dea, deae, f.	goddess	**intereā**	meanwhile		
nūntius, -ī, m.	messenger, message	**nunc**	now		
oculus, -ī, m.	eye				
imperium, -ī, n.	order				
amor, amōris, m.	love	*conjunctions*			
hiems, hiemis, f.	winter	**aut ... aut**	either ... or		

Īnfēlīx Dīdō

ubi Aenēās fīnem dīcendī facit, omnēs tacitī sedent. tandem Dīdō hospitēs dīmittit. mox omnēs dormiunt. sed Dīdō dormīre nōn potest. per tōtam noctem Aenēam et labōrēs Trōiānōrum in animō volvit.

5   Aenēās et Trōiānī post tantōs labōrēs valdē fessī sunt. eīs placet in Libyā manēre et quiēscere. intereā Dīdō Aenēam amāre incipit; Aenēam semper spectat; Aenēam etiam absentem audit et videt. neque Aenēās amōrem Dīdōnis spernit. per tōtam hiemem in Libyā manet et Dīdōnem iuvat, dum novam urbem aedificat.

10   sed rēx deōrum, Iuppiter, Aenēam dē caelō spectat in Libyā cessantem. īrātus est quod Aenēās, fātī immemor, ibi manet. Mercurium, nūntium deōrum, vocat et 'ī nunc, Mercurī,' inquit, 'ad Libyam volā. Aenēam iubē statim ad Italiam nāvigāre.'

    Mercurius patris imperia perficere parat; tālāria induit et dē 15 caelō in Libyam volat. Aenēam invenit arcem aedificantem. eī accēdit et 'audī mē, Aenēā,' inquit; 'ego sum Mercurius, deōrum nūntius; Iuppiter, rēx hominum et pater deōrum, mē mittit ad tē; mē iubet haec tibi dīcere: nōlī diūtius in Libyā manēre, fātī immemor. statim ad Italiam nāvigā et novam Trōiam ibi conde.'

20   Aenēās, ubi Mercurium ante oculōs videt et monitum Iovis audit, territus est. nōn potest imperia deōrum neglegere. ad comitēs redit et iubet eōs nāvēs parāre.

fīnem dīcendī end of speaking
hospitēs guests

volvit turns over

incipit begins
absentem absent, away
spernit despises

cessantem lingering
fātī immemor forgetful of his destiny
volā fly!
tālāria induit he puts on his winged sandals; **arcem** the citadel
aedificantem building

haec this; **diūtius** any longer

monitum Iovis the warning of Jupiter
neglegere neglect

sed Dīdō omnia cognōvit; Aenēam arcessit et 'perfide,' inquit,
'tūne parās tacitus discēdere ā meā terrā? sīc amōrem meum
25 spernis? sīc mē relinquis moritūram?' ille penitus commōtus
'neque amōrem tuum' inquit 'spernō nec tacitus abīre parō. sed
Iuppiter ipse mē iubet Italiam petere et novam Trōiam ibi
condere. Italiam nōn sponte petō.' tum vērō exardēscit Dīdōnis
īra: 'ego tē nōn retineō. ī nunc. Italiam pete. sed tē moneō: poena
30 dīra tē manet; sērius ōcius aut ego aut posterī ultiōnem tibi
exigent.' sīc dīcit et ad terram dēcidit exanimāta.

cognōvit has learnt
arcessit sends for; **perfide** traitor!
spernis do you despise?
moritūram doomed to die
penitus deeply
sponte of my own will
tum vērō then indeed
exardēscit flares up
retineō hold back
poena dīra a terrible punishment
manet awaits
sērius ōcius sooner or later
posterī my descendants
ultiōnem vengeance
tibi exigent will exact from you
exanimāta in a faint

Word-building

What do the following pairs of words mean?

verbs	nouns
gaudeō	gaudium, -ī, *n.*
imperō	imperium, -ī, *n.*
aedificō	aedificium, -ī, *n.*
amō	amor, amōris, *m.*
clāmō	clāmor, clāmōris, *m.*
timeō	timor, timōris, *m.*
labōrō	labor, labōris, *m.*
terreō	terror, terrōris, *m.* (territus, -a, -um)

Mors Dīdōnis

Translate the first paragraph and answer the questions on the other two

Aenēās trīstis et commōtus Dīdōnem relinquit et redit ad comitēs.
imperia deōrum perficere dēbet. nāvēs parātae sunt. postrīdiē
prīmā lūce Trōiānī nāvēs solvunt.

    Dīdō, ubi diēs venit, ad mare spectat. nāvēs Trōiānōrum videt
5 ad Italiam nāvigantēs. dēspērat. servōs iubet magnam pyram
exstruere. pyram ascendit. gladium capit et, dum omnēs eam
territī spectant, pectus trānsfīgit. illī, ubi Dīdōnem mortuam
vident, valdē commōtī sunt. rēgīnam lūgent et trīstēs pyram
succendunt. fūmus ad caelum surgit.
10   intereā Aenēās, dum per mare festīnat, ad Libyam respicit.
fūmum videt in caelum surgentem. 'quid videō?' inquit; 'cūr
fūmus ad caelum sīc surgit?' sed redīre nōn potest. trīstis et
ānxius Italiam petit.

prīmā lūce at first light
solvunt cast off
nāvigantēs sailing; **pyram** a pyre
exstruere to build up
gladium sword
pectus (acc.) heart; **trānsfīgit** pierces
lūgent mourn
succendunt light; **fūmus** smoke
respicit looks back
surgentem rising

1 What does Dido see when day comes? [3]
2 How does she feel? [2]
3 What does she do? [5]
4 What does Aeneas see when he looks back to Libya? [2]
5 Why is he sad and anxious? [3]
6 Do you approve of or condemn Aeneas' behaviour? [5]

Fābella: Aenēās Dīdōnem dēserit

Persōnae: Aenēās, Faber prīmus, Faber alter, Faber tertius,
    Mercurius, Trōiānus prīmus, Trōiānus alter, Dīdō

    Aenēās in lītore Libyae cessat; Carthāginis arcem Dīdōnī
    aedificat.

faber workman
alter second; **tertius** third
cessat is lingering; **arcem** citadel

5   **Aenēās**: festīnāte, fabrī. saxa ad mediam urbem portāte arcemque
    aedificāte.

mediam urbem the middle of the city

  Faber prīmus: semper saxa portāmus. fessī sumus.

  Aenēās: nōlīte cessāre, fabrī. arcem dēbēmus cōnficere rēgīnae.

cōnficere finish

  Faber alter: nōn possumus diūtius labōrāre. merīdiēs est. mihi

merīdiēs midday

10   placet sub arbore iacēre et dormīre.

arbore tree

  Aenēās: quō abītis? redīte. iubeō vōs illa saxa portāre.

quō? where to?

  Faber tertius: nōn tū nōs regis, sed Dīdō. Dīdō semper nōs iubet
    merīdiē dormīre.

  Aenēās: abīte, hominēs, paulīsper; sed celeriter redīte et arcem

paulīsper for a little while

15   mihi cōnficite.

    abeunt fabrī. Aenēās sōlus in lītore sedet. Mercurius subitō
    Aenēae appāret nūntiumque Iovis eī dat.

appāret appears; **Iovis** of Jupiter

  Mercurius: Aenēā, quid facis? cūr in lītore Libyae cessās, fātī
    immemor, et Dīdōnī urbem aedificās?

fātī immemor forgetful of your destiny

20   **Aenēās**: quis mihi dīcit? deus an homō?

an or

  Mercurius: ego Mercurius sum, deōrum nūntius.
    Iuppiter, pater deōrum et rēx hominum,
    mē mittit ad tē.

  Aenēās: cūr tē mittit Iuppiter? quid mē

25   facere iubet?

  Mercurius: Iuppiter tibi īrātus est, quod in
    Libyā cessās. iubet tē ad Italiam
    festīnāre novamque urbem
    Trōiānīs condere.

Mercury,
the messenger
of Jupiter

30   *Mercurius ēvānēscit. Aenēās territus est.*   **ēvānēscit** vanishes

Aenēās: quid facere dēbeō? nōn possum deōrum imperia
neglegere. ad comitēs festīnāre dēbeō eōsque iubēre
nāvēs parāre.

Aenēās ad comitēs festīnat. illī in lītore quiēscunt.

35   **Aenēās**: audīte, comitēs. nāvēs parāte. dēbēmus statim ā Libyā
nāvigāre.

Trōiānus prīmus: quid nōbīs dīcis, Aenēā? fessī sumus. cupimus
in Libyā manēre. nōlī nōs iubēre iterum in marī labōrāre.

Aenēās: tacē, amīce. Iuppiter ipse nōs iubet ad Italiam nāvigāre   **ipse** himself
40   novamque Trōiam condere.

Trōiānus alter: quid nōbīs dīcis? Iuppiter ipse nōs iubet novam
Trōiam in Italiā condere? gaudēte, comitēs. nec ventōs
nec tempestātēs timēmus. festīnāte ad lītus et nāvēs
celeriter parāte.

45   *exeunt Trōiānī laetī. Aenēās sōlus et trīstis in lītore manet.*

Aenēās: quid facere dēbeō? Dīdō mē amat. quōmodo possum eī   **quōmodo**? how?
dīcere imperia deōrum? quōmodo possum eam dēserere?   **dēserere** desert

sed Dīdō omnia iam cognōvit; misera et īrāta Aenēam   **cognōvit** has learnt
exspectat. ubi ille advenit, furor et īra animum eius superant.   **furor** madness; **eius** her
        superant overcome
50   **Dīdō**: perfide, tūne temptās tacitus abīre? neque amor meus tē   **perfide** traitor!; **temptās** you try
retinet nec fidēs tua? mē dēseris? mē sōlam relinquis,   **fidēs** faithfulness
moribundam?   **moribundam** to die

Aenēās: nōlī mē culpāre, Dīdō. invītus tē relinquō. invītus   **culpāre** blame; **invītus** unwilling(ly)
Italiam petō.

55   **Dīdō**: perfide, sīc tū meās lacrimās spernis? sīc tū omnia mea   **lacrimās** tears
beneficia rependis? ī nunc. ego tē nōn retineō. Italiam   **spernis** do you despise
pete. novam urbem Trōiānīs conde. sed haec tē moneō: **beneficia** kindnesses
quod tū mē prōdis amōremque meum spernis, ultiōnem   **rependis** do you repay?
dīram exspectā. sērius ōcius aut ego aut posterī poenās   **prōdis** you betray
60   tibi exigent.   **ultiōnem dīram** a terrible vengeance
        poenās ... exigent will exact
Dīdō ad terram dēcidit, exanimāta. Aenēās trīstis et ānxius ad   punishment
comitēs redit nāvēsque parat.   **exanimāta** in a faint

Dido and Aeneas

FROM AENEAS TO ROMULUS

After abandoning Dido, Aeneas eventually came to the area in central Italy where Rome now stands. He had to fight a series of terrible battles with the local tribes, the Latins, but at last he managed to win peace. His travels were finally over and he married a Latin princess called Lavinia. The Trojans now called themselves Latins and built a settlement called Lavinium after Aeneas' new wife. We are now studying the language and culture of these Italian Trojans.

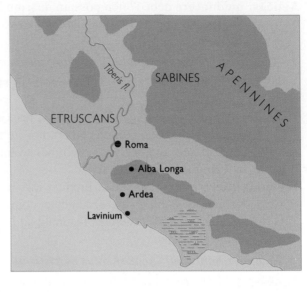

When Aeneas died, Ascanius, his son by his first marriage, became ruler. After a time, Ascanius left his step-mother to rule in Lavinium and founded his own settlement in the Alban hills, Alba Longa. Thirteen generations later, the rightful king Numitor was driven from the throne by his younger brother, Amulius. Numitor's sons were killed and his daughter, Rhea Silvia, was made a Vestal Virgin. This appeared to be an honour, but, since it meant that she was not allowed to marry, it was Amulius' way of making sure that she had no heirs.

However, the gods took an interest in this new nation, which they had destined to rule the world. Mars, the god of war, made love to Rhea Silvia who gave birth to twin boys. Understandably Amulius was furious. He imprisoned the mother and condemned the sons to be drowned in the river Tiber.

However, the river was flooded and it proved impossible to reach its main current. So the boys were left in a basket by the

A personification of the river Tiber

edge of the flood-water which, it was thought, would now sweep them away. But the waters in fact went down and the twins were found by a she-wolf who gave them milk and licked them as if they were her own cubs. The king's herdsman came upon this strange scene and took the boys to his hut. He and his wife brought them up and gave them the names of Romulus and Remus.

When they grew up, they killed Amulius and brought back their grandfather Numitor as ruler of Alba Longa in his place. But they wanted to found a new settlement on the spot where they had been left to die and then been saved by the she-wolf. There were seven hills here above the river Tiber.

The wolf with Romulus and Remus

However, since the young men were twins, it was unclear who should be king of the new settlement and they decided to consult the gods. Remus, standing on the Aventine Hill, received the sign of six vultures, but Romulus, who took his stand on the Palatine Hill, then saw twelve.

The matter was not settled, since Remus' sign had appeared first but Romulus' was double his brother's in number. Remus then provoked his brother by jumping over the small wall he was building. Romulus, in a rage, struck him over the head with his spade and killed him. 'May all who leap over my walls perish thus!' he exclaimed.

The new city was called Rome after Romulus, and the traditional date of its founding is 753 BC. It was right that Rome should prove outstanding in war, since Romulus was the son of Mars. But it was likely that much strife would follow, as he had committed the terrible crime of killing his brother.

Read the story of the birth of Moses in the Bible (Exodus, chapter 2, verses 1 to 10). Compare this story with the story of Romulus and Remus.

Cupīdō, dum Psȳchē sōla sub arbore dormit, accēdit.

dum dormit puella, Cupīdō eam tollit vehitque per aurās.

Psȳchē, ubi ēvigilat, attonita est, quod vōcēs audit sed nēminem videt.

Psȳchē, quae vultum (*the face*) marītī vidēre valdē cupit, lucernam (*a lamp*) parat.

Vocabulary 13

verbs			nouns			adverbs	
ēvigilō, -āre	I wake up		**aura, -ae**, f.	breeze, air		**numquam**	never
excitō, -āre	I rouse, awaken		**domina, -ae**, f.	mistress		**umquam**	ever
invideō, -ēre + dat.	I envy		**fōrma, -ae**, f.	shape, beauty			
teneō, -ēre	I hold		**marītus, -ī**, m.	husband		*conjunction*	
colō, -ere	I worship; I till		**sonus, -ī**, m.	sound		**sī**	if
dēpōnō, -ere	I put down		**arbor, arboris**, f.	tree			
vīvō, -ere	I live		**lūx, lūcis**, f.	light			
			vōx, vōcis, f.	voice			

adjectives				
dīvīnus, -a, -um	divine		*pronouns*	
nūllus, -a, -um	no		**nēmō, nēminis**, c.	no one
pulcher, pulchra, pulchrum	beautiful		**quī, quae, quod**	who, which

Fābula trīstis

Horātia et Scintilla sub arbore quiēscunt. Horātia mātrī dīcit: 'dum
quiēscimus, māter, nārrā mihi fabulam.' Scintilla fīliae respondet:
'quālem fābulam audīre cupis, cāra fīlia?' Horātia 'nārrā mihi'
inquit 'fābulam dulcem, māter.' Scintilla 'audī, fīlia,' inquit,
5 'nārrābō tibi fābulam dulcem sed trīstem.'

    multīs abhinc annīs in terrā longinquā rēx et rēgīna habitant quī
trēs fīliās habent; omnēs fīliae pulchrae sunt, sed nātū minima,
Psȳchē nōmine, multō pulcherrima est. omnēs virī omnēsque
fēminae eam laudant et quasi deam colunt. tandem dea Venus īrāta
10 est; invidet puellae, quod pulchra est, invidet, quod omnēs eam
quasi deam colunt. Cupīdinem arcessit et 'tū, cāre fīlī,' inquit,
'amōrem in pectoribus hūmānīs excitāre potes. ī nunc, puellam
pulchram quaere Psȳchēn nōmine. sagittam ēmitte et cōge eam
amāre hominem aliquem miserum et īnfōrmem.'
15   Cupīdō mātris imperia perficere parat. arcum capit et sagittās,
et ad terrās volat. mox Psȳchēn invenit, quae sōla sub arbore
sedet. trīstis est; nam omnēs eam laudant, omnēs colunt, sed nēmō
amat, nēmō in mātrimōnium dūcit. Cupīdō diū fōrmam illam
mīrandam spectat. iam dormit Psȳchē. accēdit Cupīdō et eam
20 propius spectat. statim amōre flagrat. dum dormit puella, tollit
eam et per aurās vehit ad domum dīvīnam; ibi eam lēniter in lectō
dēpōnit.
    mox ēvigilat Psȳchē et surgit. omnia spectat. vōcēs audit sed
nēminem videt. vōcēs dīcunt: 'omnia quae vidēs, domina, marītus
25 tuus tibi dat. nōs tibi famulae sumus. intrā et cēnā.' Psȳchē valdē
attonita est sed cēnāculum intrat et cēnam videt parātam.

quālem? what sort of?
dulcem sweet
nārrābō I shall tell

multīs abhinc annīs many years ago
longinquā far off
nātū minima the youngest
multō pulcherrima far the most beautiful
quasi like, as if
arcessit sends for
pectoribus hūmānīs human hearts
Psȳchēn (Greek accusative)
sagittam arrow; **cōge** compel!
aliquem some; **īnfōrmem** ugly
arcum his bow; **volat** flies
mātrimōnium marriage
mīrandam marvellous
propius nearer
amōre flagrat burns with love
vehit carries
lēniter gently; **in lectō** on a bed
quae (n. pl.) which, that
famulae servants
cēnāculum dining room

Psyche's divine palace

laeta cēnat. deinde dormit. dum dormit, sonum audit; ēvigilat; territa est. marītus ignōtus adest; lectum ascendit et Psȳchēn amplexū tenet; sed ante sōlis ortum discēdit. Psȳchē, ubi ēvigilat, 30 sōla est; marītī nūllum vestīgium videt. vōcēs sōlae adsunt, quae eam cūrant.

amplexū in his embrace
sōlis ortum sunrise
vestīgium trace

Respondē Latīnē

1 cūr dea Venus Psȳchae invidet?
2 cūr trīstis est Psȳchē?
3 quō vehit Cupīdō Psȳchēn?
4 ubi ēvigilat Psȳchē, quid audit?
5 quid dīcunt vōcēs illae?

Word-building

What do the following pairs of words mean?

adjectives	nouns
laetus, -a, -um	laetitia, -ae, *f.* happiness
amīcus, -a, -um	amīcitia, -ae, *f.* friendship
trīstis, trīste	trīstitia, -ae, *f.* sadness
dīligēns, dīligentis	dīligentia, -ae, *f.* care, hardwork
prūdēns, prūdentis	prūdentia, -ae, *f.* common sense

Psȳchē marītum perdit

perdit loses

Translate the first paragraph and answer the questions on the second

proximā nocte dum dormit Psȳchē, iterum adest marītus ille et 'Psȳchē,' inquit, 'uxor cāra, ego tē valdē amō et tibi omnia dō quae cupis. sed nōn licet tibi vultum meum vidēre. sī mē in lūce vīderis, numquam ad tē redībō.' Psȳchē, ubi marītī verba audit, 5 valdē trīstis est, sed ōscula marītī cōnsōlātiōnem eī ferunt. mox dormit, et ubi ēvigilat, sōla est.
Psȳchē diū sīc vīvit: interdiū vōcēs eam cūrant, nocte gaudet complexibus marītī. sed valdē cupit vultum marītī spectāre.

proximā nocte the next night

licet tibi it is allowed for you, you may
vultum face; **sī ... vīderis** if you see
redībō I shall return
ōscula kisses; **cōnsōlātiōnem** comfort
interdiū in the day time
complexibus in the embraces

itaque nocte quādam lucernam parat. marītus redit et lectum
10 ascendit; Psȳchēn complexibus ardentibus tenet, deinde dormit.
Psȳchē ē lectō exsilit lucernamque accendit; tum prīmum marītī
vultum videt. statim amōre flagrat; Cupīdinem dormientem
iterum atque iterum bāsiat. sed lucerna illa stillam oleī ardentis
ēmittit, quae in Cupīdinem cadit. statim exsilit Cupīdō, neque
15 umquam posteā ad Psȳchēn redit.

nocte quādam one night
lucernam lamp; lectum bed
complexibus ardentibus in burning
  embraces
exsilit jumps out; accendit lights
amōre flagrat she burns with love
dormientem sleeping; atque and
bāsiat kisses; stillam oleī ardentis a
  drop of burning oil
posteā afterwards

1 Describe what Psyche's
    life is like. [4]
2 Why does she prepare
    a lamp? [2]
3 What happens when she
    lights her lamp? [4]
4 What wakes Cupid? [2]
5 What does he do when
    he awakes? [3]

Cupid and Psyche

THE OLYMPIAN GODS

The ordinary Romans, especially the country people, were deeply
religious. The ancient native religion was a form of animism –
that is to say they worshipped not gods in human form but the
spirits which they believed were present in the world, e.g. the
Lares, the spirits of dead ancestors, the Penates, the spirits of the
larder, Vesta, the spirit of the hearth, etc. This religion will be
discussed further in chapter 14 when Quintus takes part in a
festival in honour of such spirits.

But the Romans fell more and more under the influence of the
Greeks and their religion. Greek religion was anthropomorphic –
that is to say they believed in gods in human form with human
characteristics. Eventually the Romans identified the Greek gods
with their own native spirits, as far as they could, and these
became the gods of the official state religion. Temples were
erected to them throughout Rome and Italy, and cults were
organized under colleges of priests.

The Greek gods were conceived as a family dwelling on Mount Olympus in north-east Greece, and so are called the Olympian gods. The twelve most important of them were:

Jupiter (Greek name: Zeus), the greatest of them all. He was the god of the sky, the weather god, who used his missile, the thunderbolt, to punish the wicked. He had to keep the rest of the gods under some sort of control and to cause what the Fates decreed to come to pass. Although a grand and powerful figure, he fell victim alarmingly often to love, and had affairs with mortal women in various disguises.

Juno, his wife (Greek name: Hera), the goddess of women and of marriage. In view of this, it is not surprising that relations between her and her frequently unfaithful husband tended to be bad!

Neptune, Jupiter's brother (Greek name: Poseidon), the god of water and of the sea, easily recognizable by his trident.

Ceres, their sister (Greek name: Demeter), the goddess of crops and fertility.

Minerva (Greek name: Athena), the goddess of wisdom and handicrafts. She sprang fully armed from the head of Jupiter and was always a virgin.

Apollo (same name in Greek), a son of Jupiter, the god of the sun, of prophecy, music and healing.

Jupiter

Minerva

Apollo

Diana, Apollo's sister (Greek name: Artemis), the goddess of hunting and childbirth. A virgin like Athena, she was also moon-goddess.

Venus (Greek name: Aphrodite), goddess of love, beauty and sexuality. She was born from the foam of the sea and eventually came to land at Paphos in Cyprus. By Mars she had a son called Cupid (Greek name: Eros), the god of physical desire.

Vulcan, Venus' husband (Greek name: Hephaestus), the lame god of fire and blacksmiths.

Mars (Greek name: Ares), the god of war. Next to Jupiter, he was the chief Italian god. He was thought to be the father of Romulus, the founder of Rome, and of his brother Remus.

Bacchus (Greek name: Dionysus), the god of wine and freedom of the spirit.

Mercury (Greek name: Hermes), the messenger of Zeus and the god of traders. He carried a herald's staff and wore a winged cap and sandals.

Diana

Venus with Mars and their son Cupid

These are the gods which appear continually in Roman literature and which were worshipped with prayer and sacrifice on state occasions. The sacrifice of animals was not just a tribute to the gods. The Romans ate much of the meat, which gave them a break from their regular cereal diet.

The public religion of the state was conducted in a highly organized manner. The high priest (*pontifex maximus*) presided over a college of priests whose main task was to advise the chief magistrates on religious matters.

It is hard to say how far the Romans of Horace's time really believed in these gods. They certainly feature prominently in art and literature and sometimes in the public speeches of politicians. But there is little evidence that they made much impact on the average Roman and nothing at all to suggest that they were a spiritual influence. In fact, it is sometimes said that the rapid spread of Christianity throughout the Roman world was partly the result of a spiritual vacuum waiting to be filled.

Mercury with the infant Bacchus

Which of the gods would you most like to be? Give your reasons.

There are many stories about the Olympian gods. What can you find out about:
  (a) the various disguises that Jupiter used to have affairs with women;
  (b) Proserpina, the daughter of Ceres;
  (c) Diana's encounter with Actaeon?

Horātia in casā sē lavat. Scintilla 'festīnā, Horātia,' inquit; 'parā tē ad cēnam.'

Quīntus amīcusque canem in agrō exercent.

puerī in hortō sē exercent. Scintilla 'quid facitis, puerī?' inquit. illī respondent 'nōs exercēmus.'

Scintilla 'festīnāte, puerī,' inquit; 'vōs parāte ad cēnam.'

Vocabulary 14

verbs		*nouns*	
lavō, -āre	I wash	**familia, -ae**, f.	family, household
exerceō, -ēre	I exercise, train	**glōria, -ae**, f.	glory
canō, -ere	I sing	**locus, -ī**, m.	place
contendō, -ere	I walk, march, hasten	**populus, -ī**, m.	people
gerō, -ere	I carry; I wear	**carmen, carminis**, n.	song
		centuriō, centuriōnis, m.	centurion
adverbs		**flōs, flōris**, m.	flower
eō	(to) there, thither	**imperātor, imperātōris**, m.	general
hodiē	today	**iuvenis, iuvenis**, m.	young man
posteā	afterwards	**legiō, legiōnis**, f.	legion
		mīles, mīlitis, m.	soldier
pronouns		**parēns, parentis**, c.	parent
is, ea, id	he, she it; that	**senex, senis**, m.	old man
quīdam, quaedam, quoddam a certain, a			
(this declines like the relative pronoun **quī, quae, quod** + the suffix **-dam**)			

A lararium. Three household gods and a sacred serpent

Parīlia

cotīdiē Flaccus prīmā lūce tōtam familiam convocat et ad
lararium dūcit. vīnum in terram fundit et Laribus supplicat: 'ō
Larēs, ōrō vōs, familiam hodiē cūrāte et pecora servāte.' deinde
ille ad agrum prōcēdit, Quīntus et Horātia ad lūdum. sed hodiē
5   Flaccus 'diēs fēstus est,' inquit; 'vōs parāte; Parīlia celebrāmus.'
    omnēs sē lavant. deinde Flaccus familiam iubet sēcum venīre
ad locum sacrum in quō Parīlia celebrāre dēbent. multī hominēs
ad agrōs laetī festīnant, virī, fēminae, puerī. Horātia Quīntusque

cotīdiē every day
lararium shrine to the Lares
fundit pours
supplicat (+ dat.) beseeches
pecora the flocks
diēs fēstus holy day
celebrāmus we are celebrating
sacrum sacred; in quō in which

[handwritten annotations: "calls together" above convocat; "care for" above cūrāte]

amīcōs salūtant. sunt multī flōrēs prope viam; puerī flōrēs carpunt

10 corōnāsque faciunt; puellīs eās dant. tandem ad locum sacrum

adveniunt. omnēs tacitī manent, dum sacerdōs vīnum in terram

fundit et Palī supplicat: 'alma Palēs,' inquit, 'tibi supplicāmus;

servā pecora, agnās cūrā, morbōs arcē.' omnēs carmen sacrum

canunt. deinde epulās parant et laetī cēnant.

15   post epulās ad lūdōs sē parant. iuvenēs magnōs acervōs

stipulae faciunt. acervōs accendunt. flammae ad caelum

ascendunt. iuvenēs fortiter flammās trānsiliunt, dum cēterī

clāmant et plaudunt.

carpunt pick	
corōnās garlands	
sacerdōs priest	
alma kindly	
agnās the lambs	
morbōs arcē keep off diseases	
epulās feast; **acervōs** heaps	
stipulae of straw	
trānsiliunt jump over	
plaudunt clap	

    dum Quīntus lūdōs spectat, accurrit Gāius et 'venī mēcum,

20 Quīnte,' inquit; 'mīlitēs in colōniam contendunt.' Quīntus,

parentum immemor, cum Gāiō ad forum currit. ubi eō adveniunt,

mīlitēs per forum iam contendunt. prīmus venit imperātor;

palūdāmentum purpureum gerit et in equō candidō vectus

exercitum dūcit; post eum equitant lēgātī. post eōs contendunt

25 centuriōnēs mīlitēsque gregāriī.

    iam multī colōnōrum ab agrīs reveniunt mīlitēsque spectant.

senex quīdam, quī prope Quīntum stat, 'ecce', inquit, 'Crassus ad

bellum prōcēdit, homō pūtidus. populum Rōmānum nōn cūrat;

nihil cupit nisi suam glōriam augēre. sine dubiō mīlitēs ad

30 mortem dūcit.' in terram īnspuit et domum abit. mox novissimī

mīlitum praetereunt colōnīque domum redeunt. sed Quīntus plūra

vidēre cupit. Gāiō dīcit: 'venī.' et post mīlitēs festīnat.

immemor forgetful of	
palūdāmentum purpureum	
a purple cloak	
candidō white; **vectus** riding on	
exercitum army; **equitant** ride	
lēgātī legionary commanders	
gregāriī ordinary, common	
pūtidus rotten	
nisi except; **augēre** to increase	
sine dubiō without doubt	
īnspuit he spits onto	
novissimī the last	
praetereunt are passing by	
plūra more (things)	

Explain the meaning of the following English phrases by reference to the Latin roots of the adjectives in bold type:

    (a) **popular** vote, (b) **juvenile** crime, (c) **military** discipline,
    (d) **parental** care, (e) **senile** folly

Word-building

What do the following words mean?

nouns	adjectives
mīles, mīlitis, *m.*	mīlitāris, mīlitāre
mors, mortis, *f.*	mortālis, mortāle
nāvis, nāvis, *f.*	nāvālis, nāvāle
rēx, rēgis, *m.*	rēgālis, rēgāle
vir, virī, *m.*	virīlis, virīle
puer, puerī, *c.*	puerīlis, puerīle
iuvenis, iuvenis, *m.*	iuvenīlis, iuvenīle
senex, senis, *m.*	senīlis, senīle

Roman soldiers

Quīntus mīlitēs spectat

Translate the first paragraph and answer the questions below on the other two

Crassus exercitum ē portīs dūcit in agrōs. tandem sē vertit et
manum tollit. exercitus cōnsistit. Crassus imperia lēgātīs dat; illī
ad legiōnēs equitant et imperia centuriōnibus trādunt. centuriōnēs
mīlitēs iubent castra pōnere. illī ad opera festīnant. ante sōlis
5 occāsum omnia parāta sunt.

    Quīntus Gāiusque mīlitēs ē colle vīcīnō spectant, parentum
immemorēs. sed Gāius 'venī mēcum, Quīnte,' inquit, 'nox adest.
domum recurrere dēbēmus. sine dubiō parentēs nostrī ānxiī sunt
et īrātī.' nox obscūra est; viam vix vidēre possunt, sed tandem ad
10 portās colōniae adveniunt.

    ubi Quīntus domum advenit, Scintilla et Horātia in casā sedent
trīstēs et ānxiae. Scintilla surgit et 'ō Quīnte,' inquit, 'ubi fuistī?
pater tē quaerit in agrīs. valdē īrātus est.' Quīntus mātrī omnia
nārrat et patrem ānxius exspectat. tandem revenit Flaccus.
15 Scintilla currit ad eum et 'Flacce,' inquit, 'Quīntus adest.
incolumis est.' Flaccus ad Quīntum sē vertit. 'ubi fuistī, Quīnte?'
inquit; 'malus puer es. cūr parentēs sīc vexās? ī nunc cubitum.'

manum hand
lēgātīs legionary commanders
opera works
sōlis occāsum sunset
vīcīnō neighbouring

sine dubiō without doubt
obscūra dark

ubi fuistī? where have you been?

vexās you worry; **cubitum** to bed

1 Why did Gaius say they must run home?   [3]
2 What was Scintilla doing when Quintus got home?   [3]
3 What was Flaccus doing?   [3]
4 What did Flaccus say to Quintus when he returned?   [5]

ROMAN RELIGION

The ordinary Romans, especially the country people, still held to
the ancient native religion. Every family worshipped the Lares,
the spirits of dead ancestors and of the farm, and the Penates, the
spirits of the larder. Each morning the father of the family
(*paterfamiliās*) would lead his household to the *larārium*, a little
shrine, often no more than a cupboard, which contained the
family *sacra* (sacred things), such as little statues of the Lares.
There he would offer gifts, incense, flowers or wine, and make
prayers on behalf of the family.

    Other gods of the home were Janus, spirit of the door (*iānua*),
who blessed the family's going out and coming in, and Vesta,
goddess of the hearth (for man cannot survive without fire), to
whom they prayed before the main meal every day.

    Every important event in life was marked by prayer and
sacrifice to the appropriate god or goddess. Birth, death,
marriage, sowing and harvest were all celebrated with religious
rituals, and there was a succession of festivals throughout the
year. Such cults meant more to the Roman countrymen than the

worship of the Olympian gods, and they believed that if they neglected these cults disaster would follow; if they observed them, they hoped all would be well. If things went wrong, they thought it was because they had offended their gods somehow. It was therefore, in a sense, a religion of fear and offered little spiritual comfort.

In this chapter Quintus and his family celebrate the Parilia, an ancient festival intended to secure the health and safety of the flocks. It was held on 21 April in honour of Pales, a deity so old that no one could say whether he/she was male or female or one god or two. The festival began with prayer and sacrifice in the fields at an altar built of turf. This was followed by a feast and a lot of drinking. Finally straw was piled up and lit; the company joined hands and jumped through the flames. No one could say just what the ritual meant but it was all good fun. It was typical of the homely, down-to-earth aspects of Roman religion.

It was a religion that encouraged superstition. Disasters like the terrible defeats at the hands of Hannibal and the Carthaginians – Dido's revenge – were apparently accompanied by strange events, as Livy records:

> Many amazing things occurred in and around the city that winter, or, as usually happens once men's minds have surrendered to superstition, many things were reported and uncritically believed. It was said that a six-month old freeborn baby had shouted 'Victory!' in the vegetable market and that an ox had climbed without any help to the third storey of a block of flats and then, terrified by the uproar from the tenants, flung itself down from there – that at Picenum it had rained stones and in Gaul a wolf had snatched a sentry's sword from its sheath and run off with it.

There was widespread belief in ghosts and werewolves, in magic spells and curses.

The priests of the state cults were elected officials. There were the augurs who had to ensure that everything the state did had the gods' approval. They achieved this by interpreting the divine messages given by the flight of birds and the feeding habits of the sacred chickens. Not everybody was impressed by the augurs. In 249 BC Publius Claudius Pulcher was preparing to fight a sea battle against Carthage. Informed of the unlucky fact that the sacred chickens could not eat, he flung them overboard saying, 'At least they can drink.' He lost the battle.

Soothsayers prophesied on the basis of the position and state of the innards of sacrificed animals – as well as strange and marvellous events (portents) and signs in the skies. These too were mocked. Cato the Elder said that he was surprised that soothsayers did not burst into giggles and give the game away when they met.

But, as we know only too well, it is easy to mock other people's religions and to misunderstand their mysteries. Because their communion ritual involved Christians in apparently eating Christ's flesh and drinking his blood, they were (reasonably, you might think) suspected in the Roman world of cannibalism. Roman religion is very hard for us to understand. A strange mixture of very different elements, it had no creed and no church. It was remarkable in the way in which it usually adapted to changing circumstances. There was little persecution. By and large men could believe what they chose and new cults were continually introduced as the Romans ranged further abroad – from Greece, Asia, Egypt and many other parts of the world. Isis from Egypt and Cybele from Asia Minor (western Turkey) became important goddesses. No one was obliged to worship these gods, but no one was prevented from joining foreign cults if they wished. The only religions to which the Romans were sometimes violently opposed were Judaism and Christianity, which denied the existence of other gods.

Eventually, after the Roman emperor Constantine was baptized into the faith in 337 AD, Christianity gained acceptance and by the end of the century it had become the official state religion.

A sacrificial procession

Describe what you see in the picture of the sacrificial procession. A purification is being performed. What animals are on their way to be sacrificed? Can you find any features of Roman religion which are shared by your religion? Can you think of any features of your religion which might have struck a Roman as strange?

What can you discover about the worship either of Isis or of Cybele?

dum Cincinnātus agrum colit, accēdunt nūntiī quī iubent eum ad senātum venīre.

ille uxōrem iubet togam prōferre festīnatque ad senātum.

ubi ad urbem accēdit, patrēs ipsī obviam (*to meet*) eī veniunt.

Cincinnātus togam dēpōnit agrumque iterum colit.

Vocabulary 15

verbs		*nouns*	
temptō, -āre	I try	**toga, -ae**, f.	toga
bellum gerō, -ere	I wage war	**auxilium, -ī**, n.	help
dēdō, -ere	I give up, surrender	**proelium, -ī**, n.	battle
repellō, -ere	I drive back	**cīvis, cīvis**, c.	citizen
circumveniō, -īre	I surround	**cōnsul, cōnsulis**, m.	consul
volō, velle	I wish, am willing	**dictātor, dictātōris**, m.	dictator
nōlō, nōlle	I am unwilling, I refuse	**moenia, moenium**, n. pl.	walls
		senātus, -ūs, m.	senate
adverbs			
haud	not	*adjectives*	
postrīdiē	the next day	**hic, haec, hoc**	this
procul	far	**ipse, ipsa, ipsum**	self
quōmodo?	how?	**pauper, pauperis**	poor
conjunction		*prepositions*	
et ... et	both ... and	**trāns** + acc.	across
		dē + abl.	about

Cincinnātus

ubi Quīntus et Horātia ā lūdō domum redeunt Flaccusque ab
agrō, omnēs quiēscunt. mox Quīntus, 'pater,' inquit, 'sī vis, nārrā
nōbīs fābulam.' ille respondet: 'quam fābulam audīre cupis,   **quam fābulam?** what story?
Quīnte?' Quīntus, 'fābulam mihi nārrā' inquit 'dē Cincinnātō,
5 pater.' ille: 'illam fābulam iam saepe audīvistī, Quīnte, sed sī tū   **audīvistī** you have heard
cupis eam iterum audīre, ego volō eam nārrāre.'

Cincinnatus

95

Cincinnātus est vir fortis et mīlitiae perītus, sed pauper; parvum agrum ipse colit trāns Tiberim. illō tempore Rōma urbs parva est; bella multīs cum hostibus semper gerit. quondam hostēs
10 exercitum in fīnēs Rōmānōs dūcunt et castra pōnunt haud procul ā moenibus urbis. cōnsul Rōmānus, vir imperītus et timidus, legiōnēs ēdūcit hostēsque repellere temptat. castra pōnit in colle prope hostēs sed timet eōs oppugnāre; illī castra Rōmāna celeriter circumveniunt et exercitum obsident.
15 ubi cīvēs haec cognōscunt, omnēs valdē timent. ad cūriam conveniunt et patrēs iubent urbem servāre; clāmant: 'urbs in magnō perīculō est. urbem servāte, ō patrēs; hostēs repellite.' cōnsul* patribus dīcit: 'quid facere dēbēmus, ō patrēs? quōmodo urbem servāre possumus?' patrēs respondent: 'Cincinnātus sōlus
20 nōs servāre potest. nam mīlitiae perītus est et vir fortis, quī patriam amat et hostēs semper vincit. eum dictātōrem creāre dēbēmus. Cincinnātum ad urbem statim arcessite.'
itaque patrēs nūntiōs ad Cincinnātum mittunt. illī trāns Tiberim festīnant et mox Cincinnātum inveniunt quī in agrō suō
25 labōrat. nūntiī ad eum accēdunt et 'Cincinnāte,' inquiunt, 'patrēs tē iubent ad senātum statim venīre.' ille attonitus est sed patrum imperia neglegere nōn potest. domum festīnat; sē lavat uxōremque iubet togam prōferre. deinde togātus cum nūntiīs ad senātum festīnat.
30 ubi ad urbem accēdit, patrēs obviam eī veniunt et in senātum dūcunt. ibi 'tū sōlus' inquiunt 'urbem servāre potes. itaque tē dictātōrem creāmus. exercitum in hostēs dūc urbemque nostram ē magnō perīculō servā.'

mīlitiae perītus experienced in war
illō tempore at that time
quondam once
fīnēs Rōmānōs Roman territory
imperītus inexperienced

cūriam the senate house
patrēs the fathers = the senators

creāre to appoint

prōferre to bring out

obviam eī to meet him

* There were two consuls; one was being besieged, the other was in charge in Rome. In an emergency a dictator was appointed who took over sole command.

Word-building

What do the following pairs of words mean?

adjectives	nouns
altus, -a, -um	altitūdō, altitūdinis, f.
longus, -a, -um	longitūdō, longitūdinis, f.
multus, -a, -um	multitūdō, multitūdinis, f.
fortis, -e	fortitūdō, fortitūdinis, f.
pulcher, pulchra, pulchrum	pulchritūdō, pulchritūdinis, f.
lātus, -a, -um	lātitūdō, lātitūdinis, f.

*Give an English word derived from each of the nouns. You have not met **lātus**; guess its meaning from the English word derived from **lātitūdō**.*

Cincinnatus solus
nos servare potest

Cincinnātus Rōmam servat

Read and understand the following passage; without translating, answer the questions below

postrīdiē Cincinnātus exercitum in hostēs dūcit. mediā nocte ad
castra hostium accēdit. deinde mīlitēs iubet hostēs circumvenīre
magnōsque clāmōrēs tollere. et hostēs et cōnsulis exercitus
clāmōrēs audiunt. cōnsul 'audīte, mīlitēs,' inquit, 'illōs clāmōrēs.
5 Rōmānī auxilium ferunt hostēsque iam oppugnant. ērumpite et
hostēs ipsī oppugnāte.' sic dīcit mīlitēsque in proelium dūcit.

   iam Rōmānī hostēs ex utrāque parte oppugnant. illī territī sunt.
dēspērant et mox sē dēdunt. arma dēpōnunt et ad fīnēs suōs
abeunt.

10 Cincinnātus mīlitēs Rōmānōs ad urbem redūcit. patrēs eum in
urbem dūcunt triumphantem. omnēs cīvēs gaudent et epulās
faciunt. sic Cincinnātus urbem servat. sed mox domum redit,
togam dēpōnit, in agrō rūrsus labōrat.

mediā nocte at midnight

ērumpite break out!

ex utrāque parte from both sides

triumphantem in triumph
epulās a feast
rūrsus again

1 When Cincinnatus approaches the enemy,
   what orders does he give?   [4]
2 What does the besieged consul tell his
   men to do?   [2]
3 Why do the enemy despair?
   What do they do?   [5]
4 How do the Romans receive Cincinnatus
   on his return?   [3]
5 What does Cincinnatus do next?   [3]
6 What moral do you think Romans might
   draw from this story?   [4]

A Roman general

FROM MONARCHY TO REPUBLIC

Rome was governed by kings for the first 244
years of its history. The names of six of these
after Romulus are recorded, and some of them
came from a talented race which lived to the
north of Rome, the Etruscans. The last king,
Tarquin the Proud, was one of these. He was a
valiant leader in war but a cruel tyrant among his
people. He added to the greatness of Rome by
carrying out vast building projects, but the
common people complained bitterly about the
labour involved, especially in the construction of
a great sewer system for the whole city.

Tarquin attacked the rich neighbouring town of Ardea in order to pay for these works. But Ardea proved extremely difficult to capture and a long siege followed. One day, Tarquin's sons were whiling away the hours drinking with their cousin Collatinus. They began to talk about their wives, each of them claiming that his own was the most virtuous and faithful. Collatinus pointed out that the only way to settle the matter was to make a sudden journey to Rome, visit their wives unexpectedly and see for themselves what they were doing.

Collatinus' idea struck the young men as a very good one. They mounted their horses and galloped to Rome, arriving there in the evening. The princes' wives were taking advantage of their husbands' absence to enjoy a lively dinner party. But they found Collatinus' wife Lucretia working with her maidservants by lamplight at her spinning. Lucretia thus was the clear winner of the competition in wifely virtue.

However, events now took a disastrous turn. One of the princes, Sextus Tarquinius, had been so overcome by the sight of the virtuous and beautiful Lucretia that he fell passionately in love with her. A few days later he paid her a visit without telling Collatinus. She received him hospitably, gave him dinner and took him to the great chamber. But Tarquinius made his way to Lucretia's bedroom at dead of night, with drawn sword. He persecuted her with dreadful threats, raped her and then rode away, proud of his shameless deed.

Lucretia now proved that she was as courageous as she was virtuous. She summoned her father and her husband and told them what had happened. Then, declaring that she could not live now that she had lost her honour, she drove a knife into her heart. Collatinus' companion Brutus drew the knife from Lucretia's body, held it up and vowed that he would drive the impious family of the Tarquins from Rome.

The dreadful story of Lucretia caused such widespread horror and indignation that Brutus found his threat easy to fulfil. In 510 BC the Tarquins were driven into exile, but they tried to regain their power, first through a conspiracy and later by force. Brutus' two sons joined in the conspiracy to bring back the tyrant, and their father had no alternative but to order their execution and watch them being beheaded. His terrible distress was obvious to all. Nevertheless, his love of the liberty which had been so recently won overcame his feelings as a father.

(The stern example of Brutus was very much in the mind of his descendant Marcus Junius Brutus 500 years later. It looked as

Brutus

99

if Julius Caesar was about to become king and bring back the hateful form of government which his ancestor Brutus had brought to an end. So he led a conspiracy to murder Caesar, his close friend.)

Tarquin then persuaded the Etruscan king Porsinna to use force to bring about his return. Porsinna advanced on Rome, but was thwarted by a number of courageous acts on the part of the Romans. The story of Cloelia which you will be reading in the next chapter is typical of the Roman's behaviour in difficult times. Porsinna stopped supporting the Tarquins. The end of the monarchy in Rome was guaranteed. The city became a republic governed by two consuls who were elected every year. The word *rēx* was from now on a hateful one to Roman ears.

Stories such as those of Lucretia, Brutus and Cincinnatus illustrate something important about the way the Romans saw themselves. Honour, patriotism and an overwhelming sense of duty were the values they most admired. An unflinching toughness in the face of adversity was the Roman ideal. All these qualities were summed up in the words *mōs māiōrum* (the custom of our ancestors). However, by Quintus' time the reality was very different, as we shall see. Almost all the great men seemed to be out for themselves.

Although the Etruscan kings had been driven out for good, the young republic faced dangers from every side, as its neighbours attempted to snuff it out. The story of Cincinnatus gives us one example of this. Within two hundred years some of these neighbours had been granted Roman citizenship, others had been admitted to a kind of half citizenship, while others had a looser alliance, keeping their independence but giving Rome charge of their foreign policy. Terrible dangers continued for Rome from enemies both in and outside Italy, but by 275 BC she controlled the whole of the Italian peninsula.

However, near the start of the first century BC, discontent among those Italian allies of Rome who did not have full Roman citizenship came to the boil. They provided a large part of the manpower of the Roman army but felt that they did not reap their proper benefit from Rome's victories. In home affairs too the Romans were liable to interfere high-handedly. And so in 91 BC Rome found herself at war with her allies (*sociī*) in what we call the Social War. Things began badly for Rome and in her highly dangerous situation she granted the allies the citizenship they desired. By 82 BC all of Italy from the Apennines southward was truly Roman.

What is your response to the story of either Lucretia or Brutus or Cincinnatus? Would it be right to call such stories Roman propaganda?

Chapter 16

Cloeliae virtus

Cloelia fēminās ad Tiberim dūcit flūmenque
trānat. *across*

Porsinna valdē īrātus est. Rōmānīs dīcit: 'vōs
foedus rumpitis; Cloeliam mihi statim trādite.'

Rōmānī Cloeliam Porsinnae trādunt, quae ad
castra hostium redit.

Rōmānī virtūtem Cloeliae honōre īnsignī
commemorant; nam statuam eius in equō
īnsidentis in Sacrā viā pōnunt.

Vocabulary 16

verbs		nouns	
līberō, -āre	I free	**statua, -ae**, f.	statue
ēvādō, -ere	I escape	**exemplum, -ī**, n.	example
poscō, -ere	I demand	**frūmentum, -ī**, n.	grain, corn
rumpō, -ere	I break	**praesidium, -ī**, n.	garrison
custōdiō, -īre	I guard	**custōs, custōdis**, m.	guard
		flūmen, flūminis, n.	river
adjectives		**foedus, foederis**, n.	treaty
dignus, -a, -um	worthy	**obses, obsidis**, c.	hostage
summus, -a, -um	highest, greatest	**pāx, pācis**, f.	peace
līber, lībera, līberum	free	**virgō, virginis**, f.	virgin, maiden
		virtūs, virtūtis, f.	courage, virtue
adverbs			
quoque	also		
nōn sōlum ... sed etiam	not only ... but also		

Cloeliae virtūs

*Translate the first two paragraphs and answer the questions
below on the rest of this passage*

postrīdiē Horātia, dum in hortō cum mātre sedet, haec dīcit: 'māter
cāra, Cincinnātus vir fortis erat et bonus. nōnne fēminae quoque
tantam virtūtem praebuērunt?' Scintilla: 'certē, cāra fīlia, multae
fēminae erant quae summam virtūtem praebuērunt, sīcut Cloelia.'
5 Horātia: 'nārrā mihi dē Cloeliā, sī vīs.' Scintilla: 'audī, Horātia.
ego tibi nārrābō dē virtūte Cloeliae.'

     erat was
     praebuērunt showed
     sīcut like

     nārrābō I will tell

multīs abhinc annīs Etruscī Rōmānōs in proeliō vincunt sed
urbem capere nōn possunt. itaque tōtam urbem circumveniunt;
praesidium in colle Iāniculō trāns Tiberim pōnunt; flūmen multīs
10 nāvibus custōdiunt. Rōmānī frūmentum in urbem importāre nōn
possunt; cīvēs iēiūnī sunt, sed fortiter resistunt neque ūllō pactō sē
dēdere volunt. tandem rēx Etruscōrum, Porsinna nōmine,
condiciōnēs pācis ipse prōpōnit: ab obsidiōne dēsistere vult sed
obsidēs ā Rōmānīs poscit. hās condiciōnēs Rōmānī accipiunt
15 obsidēsque Porsinnae trādunt. Etruscī exercitum ā Iāniculō
dēdūcunt et castra haud procul rīpā Tiberis pōnunt.

     multīs abhinc annīs many years ago

     iēiūnī starving
     ūllō pactō on any terms
     condiciōnēs conditions
     ab obsidiōne dēsistere to cease from
       the siege

     inter obsidēs sunt plēraeque fēminae. ūna ex hīs, virgō nōmine
Cloelia, ē manibus hostium ēvādere cōnstituit. custōdēs fallit, ē
castrīs effugit, manum fēminārum ad Tiberim dūcit. flūmen trānat
20 omnēsque fēminās in urbem incolumēs dūcit. prīmum Porsinna
valdē īrātus est Rōmānōsque iubet omnēs obsidēs sibi reddere.
deinde ab īrā dēsistit et, in admīrātiōnem Cloeliae virtūtis versus,
haec Rōmānīs dīcit: 'vōs foedus rumpitis, sed sī Cloeliam mihi

     plēraeque several
     ē manibus from the hands
     fallit deceives; **manum** a band
     trānat she swims across

     dēsistit he ceases from
     versus changing to

reddideritis, nōn modo eam incolumem servābō sed etiam cēterās
25 fēminas līberābō.' Rōmānī haec accipiunt Cloeliamque trādunt,
quae ad castra hostium libēns redit. Porsinna cēterās fēminās
līberat. sīc pāx redintegrāta est.

Rōmānī Cloeliae virtūtem honōre īnsignī commemorant, nam
statuam eius in summā Sacrā viā pōnunt in equō īnsidentis.

30 'Cloeliae fābula, Horātia, haec nōs docet: nōn sōlum virī sed
fēminae quoque summam virtūtem praebēre possunt summōque
honōre dignae sunt.'

sī ... reddideritis if you give back
servābō I shall keep
līberābō I shall free
libēns willing(ly)
redintegrāta renewed
honōre īnsignī with an exceptional
   honour
commemorant they commemorate
eius ... īnsidentis of her sitting on

1 What did Cloelia decide to do?   [2]
2 How did she escape to Rome?   [5]
3 What did Porsinna at first demand? Why did he change
    his mind and what terms did he offer?   [7]
4 How did the Romans honour Cloelia?   [3]
5 According to Scintilla, what does this story prove?   [2]

Word-building

What is the meaning of the following pairs of words?

dignus, -a, -um   dignitās, dignitātis, *f.*
līber, lībera, līberum   lībertās, lībertātis, *f.*
ānxius, -a, -um   ānxietās, ānxietātis, *f.*
mortālis, -e   mortālitās, mortālitātis, *f.*
celer, celeris, celere   celeritās, celeritātis, *f.*

Give an English word derived from each of the nouns listed above.

The river Tiber in Rome

HANNIBAL

One of the darkest times in the history of Rome came in the third century BC when Carthage came close to destroying her. As you may remember, Queen Dido had laid a terrifying threat of revenge upon Rome when Aeneas, the founder of the Roman nation, had abandoned her. Her words were fulfilled in a dreadful way.

The conflict with the Carthaginians was renewed three times in what are called the three Punic Wars (Punic = Carthaginian). In the first the Romans achieved victory and showed their usual rugged determination. When Horace was told about it, he was particularly impressed by the courage of Regulus, a Roman general. Regulus was captured by the Carthaginians and sent by them to Rome to negotiate an exchange of prisoners and, if possible, peace. When he arrived in Rome, he said the exact opposite of what the Carthaginians wanted him to. He told the Romans on no account to exchange prisoners but to fight on until they won. He then refused to remain in the city since he had promised to return to the place of his captivity. He was cruelly tortured to death when he arrived back in Carthage.

The Romans gained the victory, but they by no means broke the might and ambition of their enemy. One of the Carthaginian generals of this war took his son to the altar and made him swear over the sacrifice undying hatred of everything that was Roman. The boy's name was Hannibal, and when he grew up he did not forget his oath.

Hannibal's march upon Rome, which began the Second Punic War (218–202 BC), has caught the imagination of the world. He decided to fight his enemy by land, attacking them by crossing the huge natural barrier of the Alps from Spain. It proved an appalling experience. He set out with 102,000 men and he arrived in Italy with only 26,000.

But he showed great heroism and skill throughout the ordeal. He placed his elephants precariously on rafts and transported his army across the swirling waters of the wide river Rhone. Then they had a nine days' journey which took them through hostile tribes, terrible storms and a most frightening landscape:

> When they set out at dawn and the column was moving sluggishly through the unending deep snow and weariness and desperation could be clearly seen on everybody's face, Hannibal went ahead of the standards and told his soldiers to halt on a ledge from which there was a vast extensive view.

He showed them Italy and the plains beneath the Alps around the river Po, and said that they were now scaling the walls not only of Italy but also of the city of Rome. The journey ahead of them would be downhill and easy. And in one or at the most two battles, he said, they would have Italy's citadel and its capital in their grasp.

An elephant

At first it seemed as if Hannibal was right. He won a series of crushing victories over the Romans, whom he simply out-generalled. Then in 216 BC he inflicted upon them the most severe defeat they had ever known, at Cannae. Perhaps 70,000 Romans were killed in this battle, and their city again seemed to be totally at the mercy of a cruel enemy.

Yet Hannibal hesitated. The leader of his cavalry, Maharbal, begged him to send him ahead to Rome. If Hannibal did so, Maharbal told him, he would be dining on the Capitol three days later. Hannibal would not let him go, however, thinking that his men had earned a rest. 'You know how to win, Hannibal,' replied Maharbal sadly, 'but you do not know how to use your victory.'

The Romans refused to admit defeat, as so often happened amid disaster. Their stubbornness was rewarded and a stalemate developed. Hannibal moved round Italy unopposed, but the Roman army sensibly refused to engage him in a pitched battle, which he would almost certainly have won. Instead, they followed him at a distance and made it difficult for him to get supplies and reinforcements.

In 207 BC the Carthaginians attempted to turn the tide of war by sending Hannibal's brother Hasdrubal over the Alps from Spain to Italy to join him. But the Romans succeeded in defeating and killing Hasdrubal before the two armies could combine. They flung his severed head into Hannibal's camp. Hannibal exclaimed, looking sadly at this grim object, 'Carthage, I see your fate!' Yet Hannibal stayed in Italy for another four years, more and more resembling a lion at bay.

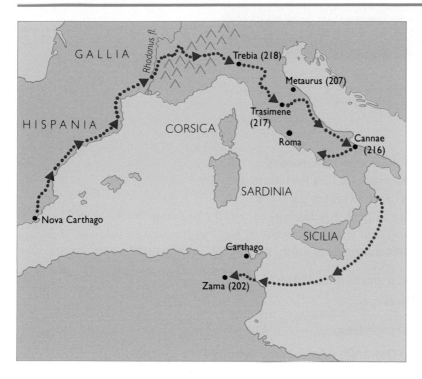

The route of Hannibal's march

Eventually the Romans made a decisive move. They sent a large Roman army to Africa to threaten Carthage itself. This meant that Hannibal had to be recalled to defend his city, and in 202 BC the Carthaginians were defeated in a great battle at Zama. The war was over and Carthage's might was shattered. Hannibal fled and some twenty years later committed suicide rather than fall into Roman hands.

Rome was now the leading power in the western Mediterranean and had won the beginnings of an empire. Yet a later generation of Romans was not content with this victory. 'Dēlenda est Carthāgō!' ('Carthage must be destroyed!') was the famous cry of Cato the Censor. The city of Carthage was razed to the ground at the end of the Third Punic War in 146 BC.

In 1985, over 2,000 years later, the Mayors of Carthage and Rome signed a peace treaty, committing the two cities to an 'exchange of knowledge and the establishment of common information, cultural and artistic programmes'.

Trace the map above and on your copy mark Hannibal's route from Spain to Italy and the sites of the principal battles.

Do you admire Hannibal? Give reasons for your answer.

Grammar and exercises

Chapter 1

NB

1 In Latin the verb often comes at the end of its sentence.
2 Latin has no word for **the** (definite article) or **a** (indefinite article);
  you must supply these in English as the context requires.
3 Latin does not always express the subject, e.g. **labōrat** by itself can mean '*he/she works*'.
4 Latin has only one form for the present tense, e.g. **labōrat**; English has two forms, e.g. 'she works' and 'she is working'. In translating from Latin, choose the form which is appropriate.

The captions illustrate two different patterns of sentence:

  1 (someone) (is doing something), e.g.

   Scintilla labōrat   Scintilla is working.

In sentences of this pattern the *verb* (**labōrat**) describes the action of the sentence, the *subject* (**Scintilla**) tells you who is performing the action.

Exercise 1.1

Translate the following

1 fēmina festīnat.
2 puella cēnat.
3 Scintilla intrat.
4 Horātia nōn labōrat.

The second type of sentence illustrated in the captions is:

  2 (someone) is (something), e.g.

   Horātia est puella   Horatia is a girl.

   Horātia fessa est   Horatia is tired.

In sentences of this pattern the verb (**est**) does not describe an action but simply joins the subject (**Horātia**) to the completing word: Horatia is – .
To complete the sense a completing word (called a *complement*) is required.
The complement may be either a noun, e.g. **puella**, or an adjective, e.g. **fessa**.

Exercise 1.2

Translate the following

1 Scintilla fessa est.
2 puella laeta est.
3 cēna nōn parāta est.
4 Scintilla est fēmina.

Exercise 1.3

In each of the following give the correct Latin form for the word in brackets and translate the whole sentence, e.g.

Scintilla ad casam (walks):   **ambulat**   Scintilla walks to the house.

1 puella in casam (enters).
2 fēmina (is working).
3 cēna nōn parāta (is).
4 Scintilla (is hurrying).
5 mox (dinner) parāta est.
6 Horātia (glad) est.

Chapter 2

The picture captions illustrate a third type of sentence pattern, e.g.

> **puella Scintillam salūtat**   The girl greets Scintilla.

Here the verb **salūtat** describes the action of the sentence; **puella**, the *subject* of the verb, tells you who performs the action, but to complete the sense we need to know whom the girl is greeting: **Scintillam**. We call this the *object* of the verb.
   Notice that the subject ends **-a**, and the object ends **-am**. So:

> **Scintill-a Horāti-am vocat**   Scintilla calls Horatia.

> **Scintill-a** is subject, **Horāti-am** is object of **vocat**.

> **Horāti-a Scintill-am vocat**   Horatia calls Scintilla.

> **Horāti-a** is the subject and **Scintill-am** the object.

The different endings in nouns (and adjectives) show what *case* they are in. The cases have names:

> The subject case, ending **-a**, is called the *nominative*.

> The object case, ending **-am**, is called the *accusative*.

Word endings must be watched with great care, since they determine the sense in Latin.

Exercise 2.1

Copy out the following sentences in Latin. Fill in the blanks with the correct endings and translate

1 Horāti– in casā labōrat.
2 puella Scintill– vocat.
3 Scintill– cas– intrat.
4 fīlia Scintill– salūtat.
5 puella cēn– parat.
6 Scintilla fīli– laudat.
7 Argus casam intrat et cēn– dēvorat.
8 Scintilla īrāt– est; cēnam iterum (*again*) par–.

Exercise 2.2

In each of the following give the correct Latin form for the word in brackets; then translate the whole sentence

1 Scintilla fīliam (calls).
2 Horātia casam (enters) et (Scintilla) salūtat.
3 Horātia Scintillam (helps).
4 Scintilla Horātiam laudat et fābulam (tells).
5 Horātia (happy) est.

Exercise 2.3

Translate into Latin

1 Horatia is carrying water into the house.
2 She is tired but she hurries.
3 She enters the house and calls Scintilla.
4 Scintilla praises (her) daughter.

Chapter 3

Latin nouns are divided into classes, called *declensions*.

1st declension nouns, with nominative ending **-a**, follow this pattern:

nominative (subject)	**puell-a**
accusative (object)	**puell-am**

2nd declension nouns, with nominative ending **-us** or **-er**, follow this pattern:

nominative (subject)	**colōn-us**	**pu-er**	**ag-er**
accusative (object)	**colōn-um**	**puer-um**	**agr-um**

Notice that there are two types of nouns ending **-er**; one type keeps the **e** of the nominative in the other cases, e.g. **puer**, **puer-um**; the other drops it, e.g. **ager**, **agr-um**.

Exercise 3.1

Translate

1 Quīntus agrum intrat et Flaccum vocat.
2 puer colōnum iuvat.
3 colōnus fīlium laudat.
4 Horātia casam intrat et Scintillam vocat.
5 puella fēminam iuvat.
6 Scintilla fīliam laudat.

Verb forms

In the first two chapters the verbs nearly all end **-at** (e.g. **par-at**); in this chapter verbs appear which end **-it** (e.g. **mitt-it**) and **-et** (e.g. **vid-et**).

Latin verbs fall into four classes called *conjugations*, which differ in the endings of their stems:

1st conjugation   stems in **-a**, e.g. **par̲a-t**
2nd conjugation   stems in **-e**, e.g. **mon̲e-t**
3rd conjugation   stems ending in consonants, e.g. **reg̲-it**
4th conjugation   stems in **-i**, e.g. **aud̲i-t**

Exercise 3.2

Pick out from the English translations below the ones which fit each of the following Latin words

1	audit	4	parat	7	redit	10	laudat
2	venit	5	vocat	8	ascendit	11	currit
3	videt	6	sedet	9	labōrat	12	salūtat

she is working, he is coming, she is returning, he climbs, she sees, he is preparing, she calls, he is sitting, he runs, she praises, he is climbing, she greets, he hears

Gender: masculine, feminine and neuter

You may already know that in French and Spanish and other modern languages, nouns are either *masculine* or *feminine* in gender. In Latin also nouns have genders.

Obviously **fīlius** (son) is masculine and **fīlia** (daughter) is feminine; but often the gender is not obvious, e.g. **cēna** (dinner) is feminine and **ager** (field) is masculine. And in Latin some nouns are *neuter* in gender, i.e. neither masculine nor feminine.

Nearly all nouns of the 1st declension with nominative ending **-a** (like **puell-a**) are feminine.

All nouns of the 2nd declension with nominative ending **-us** (like **colōn-us**) and **-er** (like **pu-er**, **ag-er**) are masculine, but there are also a fair number of neuter nouns; these have nominative and accusative **-um** e.g. **bell-um**.

Neuter nouns are not used regularly until chapter 10 but you should be aware of their existence.

Exercise 3.3

Give the gender (masculine or feminine or neuter) of the following words (which are all in the nominative case)

terra, **puer**, **via**, **saxum**, **fābula**, **colōnus**, **bellum**

Adjectives

Adjectives have masculine, feminine and neuter endings, and will be given in the vocabulary with all three genders, e.g.

masc.	*fem.*	*neuter*	
magn-us	**magn-a**	**magn-um**	big

(this is abbreviated to: **magnus**, **-a**, **-um** in vocabulary lists).

The case endings for the masculine are the same as those of **colōn-us**,
those of the feminine the same as those of **puell-a**,
those of the neuter the same as **bell-um**.

Agreement of adjectives

Adjectives always *agree with* the nouns they describe, i.e. they have the same case and gender, e.g.
puella bona, **puer laetus**, **puellam fessam**, **puerum īrātum**, **bona cēna**, **bellum longum**.

The complement after the verb **est** always agrees with the subject, e.g.
puella laeta est. **puer fessus est**.

Exercise 3.4

Correct the following Latin sentences

1 fīlia fessus est.
2 fīlius laeta est.
3 cēna nōn parātus est.
4 puer īrāta est.
5 fābula nōn longus est.

Exercise 3.5

*Complete the following sentences by giving the correct Latin for the English word in brackets,
and translate. For instance:*

Quīntus ad terram (falls); **Flaccus** (anxious) **est**. **cadit**; **ānxius**

Quintus falls to the ground; Flaccus is anxious.

1 Scintilla (a story) nārrat; fīlia (happy) est.
2 Flaccus fīlium (praises); Quīntus (happy) est.
3 puer (the farmer) vocat; colōnus (the boy) nōn audit.
4 puella Scintillam (sees); Scintilla (angry) est.
5 Quīntus diū (is working); puer (tired) est.

Chapter 4

Singular and plural

Verbs, nouns and adjectives have different sets of endings for *singular* (one person/thing)
and *plural* (more than one).

MEMENTO: If the verb ends **-t**, it is singular; if it ends **-nt**, it is plural.

As examples of verbs of each conjugation, we use:

1st conjugation	**parat**	he/she prepares
2nd conjugation	**monet**	he/she warns, advises
3rd conjugation	**regit**	he/she rules
4th conjugation	**audit**	he/she hears

Verbs

	3rd person singular	3rd person plural
1st conjugation	**para-t** he/she prepares	**para-nt** they prepare
2nd conjugation	**mone-t** he/she warns	**mone-nt** they warn
3rd conjugation	**regi-t** he/she rules	**reg-unt** they rule
4th conjugation	**audi-t** he/she hears	**audi-unt** they hear
	es-t he/she is	**su-nt** they are

Exercise 4.1

Give the plural of the following verb forms

nārrat, mittit (3), **sedet, dormit** (4), **videt, intrat**

narrant   mittunt   sediunt   vident   intrant
dormiunt

Nouns

			singular	plural
nominative	1st decl.	(*fem.*)	puell-a	puell-ae
	2nd decl.	(*masc.*)	colōn-us	colōn-ī
			puer	puer-ī
accusative	1st decl.	(*fem.*)	puella-m	puell-ās
	2nd decl.	(*masc.*)	colōn-um	colōn-ōs
			puer-um	puer-ōs

Exercise 4.2

Give the plural of the following noun plus adjective phrases
(notice that some are in the nominative, others in the accusative case)

fēmina laeta, colōnum īrātum, puer fessus, puellam miseram, agrum magnum.

fēminae laetae, colōnōs irātōs, puerī fessī, puellās miserās, agrōs magnōs

Exercise 4.3

Put into the plural and translate; for instance:

puer puellam vocat: **puerī puellās vocant**   The boys call the girls.

1	puellae puerōs vident	6	colōnī filiōs dūcunt
2	puerī fēminās audiunt	7	illa fēmina eum iuvat
3	fēminae filiōs laudant	8	puellae urnās magnās portant
4	puellae fessae sunt.	9	puerī puellās vident
5	puerī labōrant	10	puellae puerōs vocant

Exercise 4.4

Pick out from the English translations below the ones that fit each of the following Latin words

1	festīnant	4	audiunt	7	vocat	10	videt
2	audit	5	adsunt	8	ascendunt	11	accēdit
3	manent	6	parant	9	currunt	12	laudant

they are preparing, he sees, they run, they hear, he is approaching, he hears, they climb,
they are present, they praise, they stay, they are hurrying, she is calling

Note on 'ille', 'illa'

ille (that man, he) and **illa** (that woman, she) are commonly used to indicate a change of subject, e.g.

> **Scintilla Horātiam vocat; illa accēdit.**
> Scintilla calls Horatia; she (i.e. Horatia) approaches.

Exercise 4.5

Translate

1 Quīntus Flaccum vocat; ille fīlium nōn audit.
2 Scintilla fīliam laudat; illa laeta est.
3 fēminae fīliās ad fontem dūcunt; illae urnās magnās portant.
4 puerī colōnōs vident; illī in agrō labōrant.

Chapter 5

Verbs: present tense, all persons

Latin changes the verb endings to show which person (I, you, he, etc.) is performing the action of the verb. (Old English did the same, e.g. I come, thou comest, he cometh.)

There are three singular persons: I, you, he
and three plural: we, you, they

The person endings are the same for all types of verb:

singular 1 **-ō** I
2 **-s** you
3 **-t** he/she

plural 1 **-mus** we
2 **-tis** you
3 **-nt** they

These endings are attached to the verb stem.

1 *1st conjugation* (stem ends **-a**)

singular		*plural*	
par-ō	I prepare	**parā-mus**	we prepare
parā-s	you prepare	**parā-tis**	you prepare
para-t	he/she prepares	**para-nt**	they prepare

2 *2nd conjugation* (stem ends **-e**)

mone-ō	I warn	**monē-mus**	we warn
monē-s	you warn	**monē-tis**	you warn
mone-t	he/she warns	**mone-nt**	they warn

3 *3rd conjugation* (stems ending in consonants)

reg-ō	I rule	**reg-imus**	we rule
reg-is	you rule	**reg-itis**	you rule
reg-it	he/she leads	**reg-unt**	they rule

4 *4th conjugation* (stem ends **-i**)

singular		*plural*	
audi-ō	I hear	**audī-mus**	we hear
audī-s	you hear	**audī-tis**	you hear
audi-t	he/she hears	**audi-unt**	they hear

Note that in the 3rd conjugation, where the stem ends in a consonant, vowels are inserted before the person ending.

Learn also the present tense of **sum**:

sum	I am	**su-mus**	we are
e-s	you are	**es-tis**	you are
es-t	he/she is	**su-nt**	they are

Since the verb ending shows what person is the subject, there is no need to give a separate subject pronoun, e.g. **par-ō** = I prepare, **monē-mus** = we warn, **audī-tis** = you hear.

Exercise 5.1

Translate

1 Flaccum iuvāmus.
2 ad lūdum festīnō.
3 Quīntum videt.
4 in viā manētis.
5 in casā dormiunt.

6 ad agrum currō.
7 puerōs monēmus.
8 cūr puellam ad agrum mittis?
9 laetī sumus.
10 miserī estis.

Exercise 5.2

Pick out from the English translations below the ones that fit each of the following Latin verb forms

1 spectāmus
2 trādit
3 emimus

4 clāmātis
5 currimus
6 maneō

7 respondent
8 dīcimus
9 estis

10 festīnō
11 audīs
12 pōnis

we run, he hands over, I am hastening, you are, we are watching, I am staying, you hear, we buy, they reply, you place, we say, you are shouting

Exercise 5.3

In each of the following give the correct Latin for the words in brackets,
then translate the whole sentence

1 quid (are you doing), puellae? cēnam (we are preparing).
2 cūr nōn (are you hurrying), Quīnte? nōn sērō (I am coming).
3 cūr in viā (are you sitting), amīcī? in viā (we are sitting), quod fessī (we are).
4 Argus malus (is); eum (I call) sed ille nōn (come back).
5 cūr nōn fābulam (are you telling)? fābulam nōn narrō quod misera (I am).

Exercise 5.4

In the following sentences make the complement agree with the subject and translate

1 cūr (miser) estis, puerī? puellae (laetus) sunt.
2 Scintilla (īrātus) est; nam puerī nōn (parātus) sunt.
3 (fessus) sumus, quod diū labōrāmus.
4 cūr (ānxius) es, Scintilla?
5 (ānxius) sum quod Horātia (miser) est.

The ablative case

This case is at present used only after certain prepositions,
e.g. **in agr-ō** = in the field, **ā cas-ā** = from the house.

		abl. singular	*abl. plural*
1st declension	(puella)	puell-ā	puell-īs
2nd declension	(colōnus)	colōn-ō	colōn-īs
	(ager)	agr-ō	agr-īs

Note that in the nominative singular of the 1st declension **-a** is short, in the ablative it is long **-ā**.

> **MEMENTO:** look out for 1st declension nouns ending with long **-ā**; these are in the ablative case.

Exercise 5.5

Give the ablative of the following noun/adjective phrases

1 puer fessus
2 magna casa
3 multae fēminae

4 puella laeta
5 colōnī miserī

Prepositions

These are words like 'into', 'in', 'from' which together with a noun expand the action of the verb, e.g.

in casam festīnat   She hurries <u>into the house</u>.

in casam tells you where she hurries to.

in agrō labōrat   He is working <u>in the field</u>.

in agrō tells you where he is working.

Prepositions expressing motion towards are followed by the accusative, e.g. **in agrum** = into the field; **ad agrum** = to the field.

Prepositions expressing place where and motion from are followed by the ablative, e.g. **in agrō** = in the field, **ab agrō** = from the field.

Note also that **cum** (= with) takes the ablative, e.g. **cum puellā** with the girl.

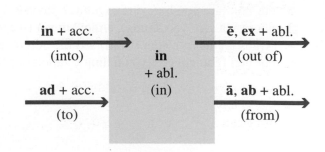

Exercise 5.6

Fill in the blanks and translate

1 Flaccus et fīlius in agr- labōrant.
2 puellae in vi- lūdunt; Scintilla eās in cas- vocat.
3 Flaccus puerōs ad agr- dūcit.
4 multae puellae cum fēmin- ad fontem ambulant.
5 puer cum amīc- ad lūd- festīnat.

Exercise 5.7

Translate into Latin

1 The farmer calls the boys into the field.
2 They stay in the field and work.
3 The boy is tired and soon returns from the field.
4 The women are walking to the house.
5 The girls are walking with the women.

Chapter 6

Infinitives

1st conjugation	parō	**parā-re**	to prepare
2nd conjugation	moneō	**monē-re**	to warn
3rd conjugation	regō	**reg-ere**	to rule
4th conjugation	audiō	**audī-re**	to hear

The infinitive is used, as in English, with verbs such as:

cupiō I desire to, want to:
> **lūdere cupimus** We want to play.

dēbeō I ought to, I must:
> **labōrāre dēbētis** You ought to work.

iubeō I order x to:
> **magister puerōs iubet labōrāre** The master orders the boys to work.

cōnstituō I decide to:
> **magister cōnstituit fābulam nārrāre** The master decides to tell a story.

Exercise 6.1

Translate

1 in viā lūdere cupimus.
2 ad lūdum festīnāre dēbētis.
3 magister puerōs iubet celeriter intrāre.
4 puerī labōrāre nōn cupiunt.
5 magister cōnstituit puerōs dīmittere.

The mixed conjugation

Besides the four regular conjugations, listed above, there is a small class of important verbs ending in **-iō** which in some forms behave like 3rd conjugation verbs and in other forms like 4th, e.g. **capiō** I take:

capi-ō	*compare*	audiō
cap-is		audīs
cap-it		audit
cap-imus		audīmus
cap-itis		audītis
capi-unt		audiunt
infinitive cap-ere		audīre

(the endings underlined are like those of **reg-ō**)

Other verbs belonging to this mixed conjugation are:
cupiō I want, desire; **faciō** I do, make.

Exercise 6.2

Replace the verb in brackets with the infinitive and then translate the whole sentence

1 puerī cupiunt puellās (iuvō).
2 sed puellae puerōs iubent ad lūdum (prōcēdō).
3 quid (faciō) cupitis, puellae?
4 cupimus in viā (maneō) et (lūdō).
5 dēbēmus in lūdō (sedeō) et magistrum (audiō).

The vocative case

A new case is used in this chapter called the *vocative*; this is used when calling or addressing someone. This case always has the same form as the nominative except for the singular of 2nd declension nouns ending **-us**, which end **-e** in the vocative.

> So, '**quid facis, Quīnt-e**?'

> But '**quid facis, Horāti-a**?' '**quid facitis, puer-ī**?'

From nouns ending **-ius** in the nominative, e.g. **fīlius**, the vocative form ends **-ī**, not **-e**,

> e.g. '**cūr dormīs, fīl-ī**?'

We sometimes find the interjection '**ō**' with the vocative,

> e.g. '**quid facis, ō fīlī**?'

Exercise 6.3

Translate into Latin

1 Why are you tired, Horatia?
2 Why are you not helping Flaccus, Quintus?
3 We are hurrying to school, Flaccus.
4 Why are you walking slowly, boys?
5 I am anxious, son.
6 Why are you angry, girls?

Questions

You have already met many sentences in Latin which are questions;
their form is not unlike that of English questions.

They are usually introduced by an interrogative (question asking) word, such as

   cūr? why?, **quōmodo**? how?, **ubi**? where? (adverbs);

   quis? who?, **quid**? what? (pronouns); **quantus**? how big? (adjective).

Sometimes the interrogative particles **-ne** (attached to the first word of the sentence) or **nōnne**
(used in questions expecting the answer 'yes') are used, e.g.

   venīs<u>ne</u> ad lūdum? Are you coming to school?

   <u>nōnne</u> ad lūdum venīs? Aren't you coming to school? *or* You are coming to school, aren't you?

Exercise 6.4

Translate

1 cūr nōn festīnās, Quīnte?
2 quis Scintillam iuvat?
3 quid facis, fīlī?
4 quantus est ager?
5 domumne mē dūcis?
6 nōnne domum mē dūcis?

Exercise 6.5

The following Latin words occur in connection with Roman education.
What do you think each word means?

1 ēdūcāre   2 schola   3 scientia   4 litterae (*also spelt* literae)   5 historia   6 grammatica

Exercise 6.6

Translate

1 amīcī ad lūdum lentē ambulant. sērō adveniunt.
2 ubi lūdum intrant, magister īrātus est.
3 'cūr sērō advenītis?' inquit; 'malī puerī estis.'
4 puerī sedent et magistrum audiunt; ille litterās docet.
5 tandem puerōs dīmittere cōnstituit; puerōs iubet domum currere.
6 puellae cum Scintillā ad fontem prōcēdunt.
7 Horātia magnam urnam portat et lentē ambulat.
8 Scintilla Horātiam festīnāre iubet. 'cūr lentē ambulās?' inquit; 'dēbēs festīnāre.'
9 ubi ad fontem adveniunt, aquam dūcunt.
10 Horātia fessa est; 'nōnne iam domum redīmus?' inquit.

Exercise 6.7

Translate into Latin

1 What are you doing, Quintus? Why aren't you helping the farmer?
2 I'm working hard; I am tired.

3 What are you doing, Horatia? We are going to market (**forum**). Aren't you ready?
4 I am ready. I'm coming quickly.
5 Flaccus tells (= orders) (his) son to come with him (**sēcum**) to the field.
6 'Quintus,' he says, 'you ought to work in the field.'
7 'Don't you want to help me?'
8 But the boy is tired; he does not want to work.
9 At last Flaccus decides to send the boy home.
10 Quintus hurries home and calls Horatia.

Chapter 7

The 3rd declension

You have so far met nouns of the 1st declension, with nominative **-a**, accusative **-am** (e.g. **puell-a, puell-am**), and the 2nd declension, with nominative **-us/-er**, accusative **-um** (e.g. **colōn-us, colōn-um; puer, puer-um; ager, agr-um**). Now nouns and adjectives of the 3rd declension are introduced.

The nominative singular has various forms, e.g. **rēx, urbs, nāvis**.
The other case endings are as follows:

	singular	plural
nominative	(varies)	-ēs
accusative	-em	-ēs
ablative	-e	-ibus

These endings are added to the noun stem. For example: **rēx** (= king), stem **rēg-**:

	singular	plural
nominative	rēx	rēg-ēs
accusative	rēg-em	rēg-ēs
ablative	rēg-e	rēg-ibus

NB
1 In the 3rd declension, the vocative is always the same as the nominative.
2 The endings are the same for nominative and accusative plural.
3 The 3rd declension contains masculine, feminine and neuter nouns, e.g. **rēx** (= king) is masculine; **nāvis** (= ship) is feminine; **mare** (= sea) is neuter.

Some nouns of the 3rd declension have nominatives ending **-er**, e.g. **pater** (= father), stem **patr-**:

	singular	plural
nominative	pater	patr-ēs
accusative	patr-em	patr-ēs
ablative	patr-e	patr-ibus

(so also **māter** mother, **frāter** brother).

Many 3rd declension nouns have stems in **-i**, e.g. **nāvis** (= ship), stem **nāvi-**:

	singular	*plural*
nominative	nāv-is	nāv-ēs
accusative	nāv-em	nāv-ēs
ablative	nāv-e	nāv-ibus

Nearly all 3rd declension nouns in **-i** decline like the nouns with consonant stems in the nominative, accusative and ablative.

Adjectives

Adjectives with 3rd declension endings have the same case endings for masculine and feminine. Most adjectives have stems in **-i** and ablative **-ī** (not **-e**), e.g. **omn-is** (= all):

	singular	*plural*
nominative	omn-is	omn-ēs
accusative	omn-em	omn-ēs
ablative	omn-ī	omn-ibus

> **MEMENTO:** the ablative of most 3rd declension nouns ends **-e**;
> but the ablative of most 3rd declension adjectives ends **-ī**.

NB

The ending of the adjective is not always the same as that of the noun with which it agrees in case and number, e.g.

> bon-**us** can-**is**, bon-**um** can-**em**, bon-**ō** can-**e**
>
> omn-**ēs** fēmin-**ae**, omn-**ēs** fēmin-**ās**, omn-**ibus** fēmin-**īs**

In these examples the endings differ since **bon-us** is 2nd declension in form but **can-is** is 3rd declension; **omn-ēs** is 3rd declension, **fēmin-ae** is 1st.

Exercise 7.1

Change the following Latin phrases into the accusative case

1 magna urbs
2 rēx fortis
3 nāvis longa
4 mātrēs laetae
5 omnēs puellae

Change the following into the ablative case

1 bonus rēx
2 puer fortis
3 omnēs comitēs
4 prīnceps trīstis
5 urbēs multae

Exercise 7.2

Complete the following sentences by filling in the blanks with the correct case ending and translate

1 Quīntus patr- vocat.
2 pater fīli- fort- laudat.
3 Horātia cum mātr- domum redit.

4 māter fīliam fess- iuvat.
5 Trōiānī urb- fortiter dēfendunt.
6 Graecī nāv- dēfendere nōn possunt.
7 Patroclus cum omn- comit- in pugnam currit.
8 omn- Trōiānī in urb- fugiunt. (acc - motion)-into
9 Hector in urb- nōn fugit sed Patrocl- oppugnat.
10 hast- iacit et Patrocl- occīdit.

Irregular verbs

Irregular verbs are verbs which do not follow the usual patterns.

possum = I am able to, I can

pos-sum	*infinitive* posse
pot-es	
pot-est	
pos-sumus	
pot-estis	
pos-sunt	

(This verb was originally **pot-sum**, but where **pot-** is followed by **s**, **pot-** becomes **pos-**.)

eō = I go

eō	*infinitive* ī-re
īs	
it	
īmus	
ītis	
eunt	

(The stem of **eō** is **i-**, and all forms of the verb start **i-**, except for **eō** and **eunt**.)

Note the following: **in-eō** I go into, **ab-eō** I go from, go away, **ad-eō** I go to, approach, **red-eō** I go back, return.

Exercise 7.3

Translate the following verb forms

1	intrō	6	sedēs	11	eō	16	possumus
2	intrāmus	7	sedētis	12	redīmus	17	potest
3	intrāre	8	sedēmus	13	abīre	18	possum
4	intrās	9	sedēre	14	ineunt	19	posse
5	intrant	10	sedeō	15	adīs	20	possunt

Exercise 7.4

Translate into Latin

1 The ships are ready; Agamemnon wants to sail now.
2 Why are you waiting? We must go quickly to the ship.
3 I cannot see the ship. Why is it not here?
4 Look! the ship is already going from the land; you cannot sail in that ship.
5 The princes order you to return home.
6 We can sail tomorrow (**crās**) in another ship.

Chapter 8

Imperatives

Imperatives are the forms of the verb used in giving orders, e.g.

> **ad agrum <u>festīnā</u>**   <u>hurry</u> to the field!
> **in casā <u>manē</u>**   <u>stay</u> in the house!
> **magistrum <u>audī</u>**   <u>listen</u> to the master!

Orders may be given to one or more persons and so Latin (unlike English) has both a singular and a plural form:

infinitive	**1** parāre	**2** monēre	**3** regere	**4** audīre
imperative sing.	**parā** prepare!	**monē** warn!	**rege** rule!	**audī** hear!
imperative pl.	**parāte**	**monēte**	**regite**	**audīte**

mixed conjugation:	*infinitive:* capere
	imperative: **cape** take! **capite**

Prohibitions, i.e. negative commands (*don't*), are expressed by **nōlī** (singular), **nōlīte** (plural) + infinitive, e.g.

> **nōlī manēre, Horātia**   Don't stay, Horatia.
> **nōlīte clāmāre, puerī**   Don't shout, boys.

> **MEMENTO:** useful tip: if you take **-re** off the infinitive, you are left with the singular imperative:
> **parā(re); monē(re); rege(re); audī(re); cape(re).**

Exercise 8.1

Translate

1 venīte ad agrum, puerī; nōlīte in casa manēre.
2 domum redī, Horātia, et Scintillam iuvā.
3 ad lūdum festīnā, Quīnte; nōlī in viā lūdere.
4 magistrum audīte, puerī; nōlīte clāmāre.
5 in casā sedē, Horātia, et fābulam audī.
6 festīnā, Horātia; ad fontem sērō prōcēdimus.
7 venīte hūc, puellae, et aquam dūcite.
8 nāvēs parāte, prīncipēs, et nāvigāte ad urbem Trōiam.
9 urbem fortiter oppugnāte et Trōiānōs vincite.
10 nōlī prope nāvēs sedēre, Achillēs, sed comitēs dēfende.

Exercise 8.2

Translate into Latin

1 Come in quickly, children, and sit down.
2 Come here, Decimus; I want to see your tablet.
3 Work hard, Julia; don't play.
4 We are working hard, master; and so tell us (**nōbīs**) a story.
5 Listen to the story, children, and don't shout.

Exercise 8.3

Match up the English translations below with the following Latin verb forms

1 parat *– she prepares*
2 cape *– take*
3 īmus *– we are going*
4 parāte *– prepare!*
5 sumus *– we are*
6 iubētis *– you order*
7 īre *– to go*
8 fugere *– to flee*

9 abīte *– go away*
10 possumus *– we can*
11 oppugnāte *– attack!*
12 posse *– to be able*
13 estis *– you are*
14 venī *– come*
15 eunt *– they are going*

come!, we are going, she prepares, attack!, to flee, they are going, prepare!,

to be able, go away!, we are, to go, you are, take!, you order, we can

Prepositions continued

Revise the prepositions you have met so far:

Followed by the *accusative*:

ad   to, towards
in   into, onto
per through
circum round
prope near

Followed by the *ablative*:

ā/ab from (**ā** before consonants, **ab** before vowels,
    e.g. **ā casā**, **ab agrō**)
cum with
ē/ex out of, from (**ē** before consonants, **ex** before vowels)
in in, on

Exercise 8.4

In the following sentences put the nouns in brackets into the correct case; then translate the whole sentence (the nouns in brackets are all in the nominative case)

1 Quīntus ad (lūdus) cum (amīcī) accēdit.
2 magister puerōs prope (iānua) lūdī exspectat.
3 ubi puerōs videt, eōs in (lūdus) vocat.
4 tandem puerōs dīmittit; illī laetī ā (lūdus) domum festīnant.
5 Quīntus et Horātia ad (ager) festīnant.
6 ubi accēdunt, Argus eōs videt et ex (ager) currit.
7 puerī cibum ad (pater) portant.
8 ille in (terrā) sedet et cibum cōnsūmit.
9 Quīntus in (ager) manet; Horātia cum (Argus) domum redit.
10 ubi Scintilla fīliam videt, ē (casa) exit et eam salūtat.

Compound verbs

Prepositions can be put before verbs to form one word; such verbs are called compound verbs, e.g.

>**mittō** I send: **immittō** (= **in-mittō**) I send into; **ēmittō** I send out.
>**dūcō** I lead: **addūcō** I lead to; **ēdūcō** I lead out; **indūcō** I lead into.

Note also the prefix **re-** (**red-** before vowels); it means 'back', e.g.

>**re-mittō** I send back, **re-vocō** I call back, **re-dūcō** I lead back, **red-eō** I go back, return.

The prefix **con-** means 'together', e.g.

>**convocō** I call together, **conveniō** I come together

>(it can also be used to strengthen the meaning of the verb, e.g. **iaciō** I throw, **coniciō** I hurl).

Give the meaning of the following verb forms

>accurrit (= ad-currit), incurrit, recurrit, concurrunt, advenit, revenit, conveniunt.

Note **-que** = 'and', e.g. **māter paterque** mother and father; **-que** is tacked onto the second of two words or phrases of a pair:

>**puerī puellaeque in viā lūdunt** The boys and girls are playing in the road.
>**Scintilla casam init cēnamque parat** Scintilla goes into the house and prepares dinner.

Exercise 8.5

Translate

1 Quīntus Gāiusque lūdum ineunt.
2 cēterī puerī iam adsunt magistrumque audiunt.
3 ille īrātus est, et 'cūr sērō advenītis?' inquit; 'inīte celeriter et sedēte.'
4 Horātia in hortum init; Scintilla eam revocat.
5 'redī, fīlia,' inquit, 'et venī mēcum ad agrum.'
6 Horātia Argum ex hortō ēdūcit recurritque ad mātrem.
7 māter fīliaque cum Argō ad agrum festīnant.
8 ubi adveniunt, Scintilla Flaccum vocat; 'venī hūc, Flacce,' inquit, 'cēnam ad tē portāmus.'
9 Flaccus accēdit cēnamque accipit.
10 Flaccus Horātiam domum remittit; sed Scintilla manet Flaccumque iuvat.

Exercise 8.6

Translate into Latin

1 Stay in the field, Scintilla, and help me, but send Horatia back home.
2 Don't send me home; I want to stay and work with mother.
3 And so they all stay and work in the field.
4 Quintus, when he returns from school, hurries to the field.
5 He runs up to (his) father and says 'I want to help you. What must I do?'

Chapter 9

The genitive case (= of)

Now you must learn the genitive case, e.g.

> **puell-ae mater**   the mother <u>of the girl</u> or <u>the girl's</u> mother
> **puer-ī pater**   the father <u>of the boy</u> or <u>the boy's</u> father.

The endings of the genitive case for the three declensions are:

	singular	*plural*
1st declension	**puell-ae** of the girl, the girl's	**puell-ārum** of the girls, the girls'
2nd declension	**colōn-ī** of the farmer, the farmer's	**colōn-ōrum** of the farmers, the farmers'
3rd declension consonant stems	**rēg-is** of the king, the king's	**rēg-um** of the kings, the kings'
i- stems	**nāv-is** of the ship, the ship's	**nāv-ium** of the ships, the ships'

Note that **i-** stems keep the **i** in the genitive plural.

> **MEMENTO**: Useful tip: if you remove the genitive ending from 3rd declension nouns you are left with the stem, e.g. **rēg-is**, stem **rēg-**; **comit-is**, stem **comit-**.

The noun in the genitive usually depends on another noun, the genitive + noun forming one phrase; as in English, it may come before or after the noun it belongs to, e.g. **colōnī ager = ager colōnī** (the farmer's field = the field of the farmer).

The possessive genitive

The commonest use of the genitive case is to express possession, e.g. **patris ager** father's field = the field belonging to father.

Translate the following phrases

> Horātiae māter,   Quīntī pater,   Graecōrum prīncipēs,   portae urbis,   nāvēs rēgum, prōrae (*the prows*) nāvium,   multī Trōiānōrum,   paucae fēminārum.

(The last two phrases illustrate a different use of the genitive, called the *partitive genitive*; this also will be translated 'of'.)

Exercise 9.1

Put the words in brackets into the genitive case and translate

1   puella fābulam (māter) laeta audit.
2   magister tabulās (puerī) spectat.

3 Quīntus ad (pater) agrum celeriter currit.
4 colōnus clāmōrēs (fēminae) audīre nōn potest.
5 multī (prīncipēs) in urbem fugere cupiunt.
6 paucī (Trōiānī) fortiter pugnant.
7 Hector ter fugit circum mūrōs (urbs).
8 omnēs Trōiānī (Hector) mortem lūgent (*mourn*).

Adverbs

Adverbs are usually attached to verbs and tell you how the action of the verb is performed, e.g.

> We are walking <u>slowly</u> **lentē ambulāmus.**

Adverbs never change their form.

Many adverbs are formed from adjectives; from **bonus** type adjectives,
they are formed by changing **-us** to **-ē**, e.g.

lent-us slow   **lent-ē** slowly
mal-us bad   **mal-e** badly
(NB **bon-us** good but **ben-e** well).

3rd declension adjectives usually form adverbs by adding **-ter** to the stem:

fortis brave   **fortiter** bravely
celer quick   **celeriter** quickly.

There are many adverbs which are not formed from adjectives, such as:

diū for a long time	**numquam** never	**semper** always
mox soon	**subitō** suddenly	**hūc** hither, (to) here
vix scarcely	**iam** now, already	**cūr?** why?
umquam ever	**tandem** at last	**quandō?** when?

Exercise 9.2

In the following sentences fill in the blank with an appropriate adverb from the list below and translate

1 — pugnāte, amīcī, urbemque capite.
2 venī —, Quīnte; pater tē — exspectat.
3 labōrāte —, puerī; magister nōs spectat.
4 Decimus litterās — scrībit; asinus est.
5 cūr — ambulās, Quīnte? — nōn festīnās?

> **lentē, male, hūc, dīligenter, cūr? diū, fortiter**

Exercise 9.3

Translate the following verb forms

1	capere	6	abīte	11	vincite
2	capimus	7	abeunt	12	vincō
3	cape	8	abīre	13	vincere
4	capis	9	abītis	14	vincis
5	capiō	10	abī	15	vincunt

Exercise 9.4

Translate into Latin

1 The woman is waiting near the gates of the city.
2 The son is leading (his) father's horse to the field.
3 The children fear the master's anger.
4 We cannot see the prows (**prōrās**) of the ships.
5 We want to hear the woman's story.
6 Can you see the girl's mother?

Chapter 10

Neuter nouns and adjectives

Remember that in Latin there are a number of neuter nouns, i.e. nouns that are neither masculine nor feminine. Note:

1 There are no neuter nouns of the 1st declension.

2 2nd declension neuter nouns end **-um** in nominative, vocative and accusative singular; **-a** in nominative, vocative and accusative plural. Otherwise they decline like other 2nd declension nouns. Thus **bellum** (war) declines as follows:

	singular	*plural*
nom., voc., acc.	bellum	bella
gen.	bellī	bellōrum
abl.	bellō	bellīs

Note the following 2nd declension neuter nouns:

caelum sky, heaven	**imperium** order
cōnsilium plan	**perīculum** danger
verbum word	**saxum** rock

3 3rd declension neuter nouns have various endings in the nominative, e.g. some end **-us**, others **-en**; most 3rd declension neuter nouns have stems ending in consonants:

lītus shore
stem: **lītor-**

	singular	*plural*
nom., voc., acc.	lītus	lītor-a
gen.	lītor-is	lītor-um
abl.	lītor-e	lītor-ibus

Note:

flūmen, flūmin-is, n. river
nōmen, nōmin-is, n. name
tempus, tempor-is, n. time

A few have stems in **-i** with ablative **-ī** (not **-e**) and these keep **i** throughout the plural, e.g. **mare** sea; stem **mari-**:

	singular	*plural*
nom., voc., acc.	mare	maria
gen.	maris	marium
abl.	marī	maribus

MEMENTO: neuter nouns of all declensions have nominative, vocative and accusative plural ending **-a**, e.g. **bell-a**, **lītor-a**, **mari-a**.

Adjectives (see charts on p. 146)

The neuter case endings of adjectives with 1st and 2nd declension endings, e.g. **bon-us, bon-a, bon-um; miser, miser-a, miser-um**, are the same as those of **bellum**.

Most 3rd declension adjectives have stems in **-i** and keep the **i** in the ablative singular, genitive plural and throughout the plural of the neuter:

	singular		*plural*	
	m. & f.	*neuter*	*m. & f.*	*neuter*
nom.	omnis	omne	omnēs	omnia
acc.	omnem	omne	omnēs	omnia
gen.	omnis	omnis	omnium	omnium
abl.	omnī	omnī	omnibus	omnibus

Exercise 10.1

Put the following Latin phrases (i) into the accusative, (ii) into the genitive, and (iii) into the ablative case. For example:

omne lītus: (i) omne lītus (ii) omnis lītoris (iii) omnī lītore

1 puer fortis
2 multa saxa
3 puellae trīstēs
4 magnum perīculum
5 silvae ingentēs
6 nāvis celer
7 altus mōns
8 omnia verba

Exercise 10.2

Translate

1 fugite, comitēs; gigantēs saxa ingentia in nōs coniciunt.   *huge*
2 nōlīte in lītore manēre sed ad mare currite et nāvēs cōnscendite.
3 tempus est celeriter rēmigāre (*to row*); iam ē perīculō incolumēs ēvādimus (*we are escaping*).
4 sed caelum spectāte, comitēs; in perīculum novum cadimus.
5 magna tempestās venit; semper nova perīcula subīmus (*we are undergoing*).

Exercise 10.3

Translate the following verb forms

1	mittit	6	facere	11	redeunt
2	mittite	7	faciunt	12	redit
3	mittere	8	facite	13	redī
4	mittō	9	facitis	14	redīmus
5	mittunt	10	faciō	15	redīre

Exercise 10.4

Translate into Latin

1 At last the Trojans arrive at Sicily (**Sicilia**) and rest on the shore.
2 But they are in great danger; Mount Aetna is hurling huge rocks into the sky.
3 Suddenly Aeneas sees Polyphemus; 'Comrades,' he says, 'run to the sea and board the ships.'
4 The Trojans hear the words of Aeneas (*gen.* **Aenēae**) and run to the ships.
5 Polyphemus hears them but he cannot see them.
6 The Trojans are safe; for they are already sailing on the open (**apertus, -a, -um**) sea.

Chapter 11

The dative case: indirect object

MEMENTO: Simple rule: dative case = 'to' or 'for'.

The dative case is most commonly used with verbs meaning to 'say to', 'give to', 'show to', e.g.

> **pater fīli-ō dīcit**   The father says <u>to his son</u>.
> **māter fīli-ae cēnam dat**   The mother gives dinner <u>to her daughter</u>.
> **rēx prīncip-ibus equum ostendit**   The king shows the horse <u>to the princes</u>.

These datives are called *indirect objects*:

> **Scintilla fābulam fīliae nārrat**   Scintilla tells a story to her daughter.

Who tells the story?	Scintilla (*subject*)
What does she tell?	a story (*object*)
Who does she tell it to?	to her daughter (*indirect object*)

The dative forms of the first three declensions are:

		singular	plural
1st declension	(**puella**)	puell-ae	puell-īs
2nd declension	(**colōnus**)	colōn-ō,	colōn-īs
	(**puer**)	puer-ō	puer-īs
3rd declension	(**rēx**)	rēg-ī	rēg-ibus
	(**nāvis**)	nāv-ī	nāv-ibus

You have now learnt all the cases; study the tables of nouns and adjectives in the Reference grammar, pp. 145–6, where the full declensions are set out.

Note also:

> **mihi** to me; **tibi** to you; **nōbīs** to us; **vōbīs** to you; **eī** to him, to her; **eīs** to them

Exercise 11.1

Put the following phrases into the dative case

1 bona puella
2 fīlius cārus
3 rēx fortis
4 mātrēs laetae
5 omnia lītora
6 parvus puer

Note that English has two ways of expressing the indirect object, e.g.

> 1 Mother gives dinner to her children.
> 2 Mother gives her children dinner.

But in Latin the indirect object is always in the dative.

Exercise 11.2

Translate the following sentences in the two different ways described above

1 dā mihi cēnam.
2 vōbīs patris equum ostendō.
3 tibi omnia dīcō.
4 prīnceps arma rēgī dat.
5 rēgīna arma eī reddit.
6 nārrā nōbīs fābulam laetam.
7 fābulam vōbīs nārrō trīstem.
8 pater fīliō canem dat.
9 fīlius canem amīcō ostendit.
10 amīcus 'canis sitit (*is thirsty*),' inquit; 'dēbēs aquam eī dare.'

Exercise 11.3

Translate into Latin

1 The woman gives water to the horses.
2 The father gives his son the food.
3 The boy returns (i.e. gives back) the food to (his) father.
4 Mother is telling the girls a story.
5 The king is showing the princes the ships.
6 The farmer hands over the dog to me.

Further uses of the dative case

1 A number of verbs take the dative, e.g.

> **tibi resistō** I resist you
> **tibi persuādeō** I persuade you
> **comitibus imperō** I order my comrades
> **mihi placet** it pleases me

(These datives are indirect objects, e.g. **resistō** <u>tibi</u> I stand up <u>to you</u>; **mihi** **placet** it is pleasing <u>to me</u>). So also **īrātus est tibi** He is angry with you.

The dative is used with many verbs of motion, e.g.

> **tibi accēdō** I approach you
> **tibi succurrō** I run to help you, I help you
> **tibi occurrō** I run to meet you, I meet you

2 Besides meaning 'to', expressing the indirect object, the dative case can mean 'for', expressing the person concerned with anything, e.g.

> **fēmina cēnam <u>puerīs</u> parat** The woman is preparing dinner <u>for her children</u>.
> **<u>mihi</u> prōpositum est terram explōrāre** It is the intention <u>for me</u> (i.e. it is my intention) to explore the land.
> **<u>mihi</u> nōmen est Quīntus** The name <u>for me</u> (i.e. my name) is Quintus.

Exercise 11.4

Translate

1 Trōiānī Graecīs fortiter resistunt; Graecī urbem capere nōn possunt.
2 Ulixēs cōnsilium novum prīncipibus ostendit; eīs imperat equum ligneum facere.
3 Agamemnōn prīncipibus dīcit: 'Ulixēs bonum cōnsilium nōbīs ostendit; mihi propositum est cōnsilium eius (*his*) perficere.'
4 Graecī equum faciunt, sīcut (*just as*) Ulixēs eīs imperat; sīc Graecī Trōiam tandem capiunt.
5 puerī dīligenter labōrant; magister praemium (*reward*) eīs dat.
6 Quīntus domum currit mātrīque omnia nārrat.
7 Horātia frātrī occurrit et ōsculum (*a kiss*) eī dat.
8 Scintilla eīs dīcit: 'festīnāte, puerī; cēnam vōbīs parō.'

Exercise 11.5

Translate into Latin

1 Horatia meets (her) mother in the road.
2 She says to (her) daughter, 'Come to the fountain and help me.'
3 When they are returning home, they meet Quintus.
4 Scintilla prepares supper for the children; then she tells them a story.
5 Dido gives a great dinner for the Trojans and the princes of Carthage (**Carthāgō, Carthāginis**).
6 When the dinner is finished, she says to Aeneas (*dat.* **Aenēae**), 'Tell us about (i.e. narrate to us) all the sufferings of the Trojans.'

Chapter 12

Review of nouns and adjectives

You have now learnt all six cases of nouns and adjectives for the first three declensions. The uses of the different cases may be summarized as follows:

> *Nominative* **1** subject of clause; **2** complement after the verb 'to be'
> *Vocative*   used only in addressing or calling someone

Accusative **1** object of a transitive verb; **2** after some prepositions (e.g. **ad**, **per** etc.)
Genitive = 'of'
Dative = 'to' or 'for'
Ablative **1** = 'by', 'with' or 'from'*; **2** used after certain prepositions, e.g. **ā/ab**, **ē/ex**, **cum**

* these uses of the ablative without a preposition are explained in Part II

> **MEMENTO**: Simple rule: the ablative case without a preposition can mean 'by', 'with' or 'from'.

Revise carefully the full tables of nouns and adjectives in the Reference grammar, pp. 145–6.

'est' and 'sunt'

You have been familiar with the verb **esse** since the very begining of this course: it is used to join subject and complement (e.g. **Quīntus est laetus; Quīntus est puer**). It can also be used without a complement, meaning 'there is', 'there are', e.g.

> **est pulchra puella in viā** There's a beautiful girl in the road.
> **sunt multī canēs in agrō** There are many dogs in the field.
> **est procul in pelagō saxum spūmantia contrā lītora** There is a rock far off in the sea, facing the foaming shores. (Virgil, *Aeneid* v, 124)

In this usage **est/sunt** usually come first word in the sentence.

Note the imperatives of esse: **es/estō** (sing.), **este** (plural), e.g.

> **fortis estō, Quīnte** Be brave, Quintus.
> **fortēs este, mīlitēs** Be brave, soldiers.

Exercise 12.1

Translate

1 sunt multa templa in urbe.
2 est ingēns saxum in illō lītore.
3 dīligentēs este, puerī, et litterās bene scrībite.
4 sunt multī canēs in illā silvā.
5 tacitus estō, Quīnte; magister tē spectat.

Exercise 12.2

Revise the prepositions on p. 124. Then in the following sentences put each word in brackets into the case required by the preceeding preposition and translate the sentences

1 Trōiānī, ubi ad (Sicilia) adveniunt, ē (nāvēs) exeunt et in (lītus) quiēscunt.
2 postrīdiē Polyphēmum vident; ille de (mōns altus) lentē dēscendit.
3 Trōiānī eī resistere nōn possunt. Aenēās comitibus imperat ad (nāvēs) fugere.
4 ubi ad (lītus) adveniunt, nāvēs cōnscendunt et ā (terra) rēmigant.
5 Polyphēmus ad (mare) advenit et per (undae) ambulat.
6 subitō Trōiānōs audit et Cyclōpibus clāmat: 'dē (montēs) dēscendite; mihi succurrite.'
7 illī celeriter conveniunt saxaque ingentia ē (lītus) in (nāvēs) coniciunt.
8 sed Trōiānī fortiter rēmigant et sīc ē (perīculum) incolumēs ēvādunt.

Exercise 12.3

In the following phrases, the words in bold type are derived from Latin words you know. Explain their meaning in English and show how the English meaning is related to the Latin root, e.g.

undulating hills = with a wave-like outline: **unda** = wave.

1 **tempestuous** seas   3 **verbal** answers   5 a **bellicose** man
2 **marine habitat**   4 an **amicable** meeting

Exercise 12.4

Translate into Latin

1 When Aeneas sees Dido (**Dīdō, Dīdōn-is**), he runs up to her and says, 'Help us, queen.'
2 Dido receives him kindly (**benignē**), for the fame of the Trojans is known to all.
3 She leads him to the palace (**rēgia**) and gives a great dinner for all the Trojans.
4 After the dinner, she says, 'Aeneas, tell us all the sufferings of the Trojans.'
5 All listen silent(ly) to him, while he tells them the story.

Chapter 13

Subordinate clauses

A clause is a group of words containing a verb, e.g. 'Flaccus calls Quintus'.
This clause forms a complete sentence.

'When Quintus enters the field ...' This group of words forms a clause, containing the verb 'enters', but it is not complete. It needs another clause to complete it:

'When Quintus enters the field, <u>Flaccus calls him</u>.'

This sentence consists of two clauses:

1 When Quintus enters the field (*subordinate clause*)
2 Flaccus calls him (*main clause*)

The two clauses are joined by the *conjunction* (= joining word) 'when'. The 'when' clause, which does not form a complete sentence, is called a 'subordinate' clause, which is joined to the 'main' (grammatically complete) clause by the subordinating conjunction 'when'.

You have met the following Latin subordinating conjunctions:

ubi when,   **quod** because,   **dum** while,   **sī** if.

Exercise 13.1

Make up five complete sentences in English which each contain a subordinate clause and a main clause; use a different one of each of the conjunctions listed above for each sentence.

Put brackets round the subordinate clause, e.g.

(When you return home,) I shall see you again.

Exercise 13.2

Translate; in your translations underline the subordinating conjunctions

1 dum Horātia quiēscit, Scintilla fābulam nārrat.
2 Horātia gaudet, quod fābula eī placet.
3 sī fābulam audīre cupis, tacē et mē audī.
4 ubi Quīntus ā lūdō redit, ille quoque (*also*) fābulam audit.
5 dea Venus puellae invidet, quod omnēs eam quasi (*like*) deam colunt.
6 dum Psȳchē dormit, Cupīdō eam tollit per auram.
7 ubi Psȳchē ēvigilat, nēminem videt.
8 Psȳchē trīstis est, quod marītī vultum numquam videt.

The relative pronoun

Another word which introduces subordinate clauses is **quī** who, which (masculine),
quae who, which (feminine), **quod** which (neuter), e.g.

> **Hector, quī fortis est, Achillī resistit.**
> Hector, who is brave, resists Achilles.

> **Psȳchē, quae valdē fessa est, mox dormit.**
> Psyche, who is very tired, soon sleeps.

> **Aenēās accēdit ad templum quod in colle stat.**
> Aeneas approaches the temple which stands on a hill.

Notice that the relative pronoun has the same gender and number as the word it refers to; and so:

> **Hector** (masculine) **quī** (masculine) …
> **Psȳchē** (feminine) **quae** (feminine) …
> **templum** (neuter) **quod** (neuter) …

The plural forms are very similar to the singular:

> masculine plural: **quī**; feminine plural: **quae**; neuter plural: **quae**; and so:

> **Aenēās multōs hominēs videt quī urbem aedificant.**
> Aeneas sees many men who are building a city.

> **Scintilla fēminās salūtat quae aquam dūcunt.**
> Scintilla greets the women who are drawing water.

> **Cyclōpēs multa saxa coniciunt quae nāvēs Trōiānōrum nōn contingunt.**
> The Cyclopes hurl many rocks which do not reach the Trojans' ships.

Exercise 13.3

Translate

1 Quīntus, quī ad lūdum festīnat, amīcō in viā occurrit.
2 Horātia, quae Quīntum exspectat, in viā sedet.
3 fēminae quae ad fontem adsunt Horātiae mātrem salūtant.
4 Ulixēs cōnsilium prīncipibus expōnit quod eīs placet.
5 Aenēās imperia Iovis (*of Jupiter*) audit, quae eum terrent.
6 Trōiānī, quī Polyphēmum iam vident, territī sunt.

7 Quīntus amīcōs, quī prope lūdum lūdunt, vocat.

8 Horātia puellīs quae ad fontem prōcēdunt occurrit.

9 prīncipēs omnia faciunt quae rēx imperat.

10 is quī (*the man who*) nōs iuvat mihi nōn nōtus est.

helps us, is not known to me.

Exercise 13.4

In the following sentences fill in the blanks with the correct form of the relative pronoun and translate

1 vidēsne illās fēminās — ad fontem festīnant? *do u see those women = quae hurrying to the fountain?*

2 Graecīs fortiter resistite *qui* urbem oppugnant. *resist the Greeks bravely — Bravely resist the Greeks, who are....*

3 caelum spectāte, *quī* iam serēnum (*clear*) est. *look at the sky*

4 nōlīte perīcula timēre, *quae* — nōn magna sunt. *don't fear the dangers*

5 Horātiam salūtā, — tē in hortō exspectat. *quī (is waiting for you in the garden)*

Exercise 13.5

Translate into Latin

1 While Quintus is playing, Horatia is working.

2 If you are playing, come here and help me.

3 I don't want to help you, because I am tired.

4 Psyche, who is sitting alone, is sad.

5 While she is sleeping, she hears a sound.

6 When she wakes up, she sees no one.

7 The Trojans sail to the shore which is nearest (**proximum**).

8 Aeneas, who wishes to explore (**explōrāre**) the land, leaves his comrades on the shore.

9 He climbs a hill and sees many men who are building a city.

10 He approaches the temples which stand in the city.

Chapter 14

Pronouns 1: demonstrative pronouns

Learn the following *demonstrative pronouns*:

is he, **ea** she, **id** it; that

| | *singular* | | | *plural* | | |
	m.	*f.*	*n.*	*m.*	*f.*	*n.*
nom.	is	ea	id	eī	eae	ea
acc.	eum	eam	id	eōs	eās	ea
gen.	eius	eius	eius	eōrum	eārum	eōrum
dat.	eī	eī	eī	eīs	eīs	eīs
abl.	eō	eā	eō	eīs	eīs	eīs

ille he, **illa** she, **illud** it; that

	singular			*plural*		
	m.	*f.*	*n.*	*m.*	*f.*	*n.*
nom.	ille	illa	illud	illī	illae	illa
acc.	illum	illam	illud	illōs	illās	illa
gen.	illīus	illīus	illīus	illōrum	illārum	illōrum
dat.	illī	illī	illī	illīs	illīs	illīs
abl.	illō	illā	illō	illīs	illīs	illīs

Note that the neuter singular nominative and accusative and the genitive and dative singular forms are irregular; the other case endings are the same as those of **bonus, -a, -um**.

ille is more emphatic than **is**, meaning 'that over there'. As we have seen, it is often used to indicate a change of subject.

Exercise 14.1

Replace the underlined nouns with the correct forms of **is** *or* **ille** *and then translate, e.g.*

> **pater fīliam vocat; fīlia ad patrem festīnat.**
>
> **pater fīliam vocat; illa ad eum festīnat.**
>
> The father calls his daughter; she hurries to him.

1 Scintilla Horātiae fābulam nārrat; Horātia Scintillam laeta audit.
2 magister puerōs lūdum intrāre iubet; puerī magistrō pārent (*obey* + dat.).
3 Quīntus amīcīs in viā occurrit; amīcī Quīntum manēre iubent.
4 Flaccus Argum vocat; Argus Flaccum nōn audit; nam dormit.
5 Horātia puellās in forō exspectat; puellae ad Horātiam festīnant.

Pronouns 2: personal pronouns

You have already met the personal pronouns (I, you etc.); we now give their full declension, and add the reflexive pronoun **sē** (himself, herself etc.):

	singular	*plural*
nom.	**ego** I	**nōs** we
acc.	**mē** me	**nōs** us
gen.	**meī** of me	**nostrī** of us
dat.	**mihi** to/for me	**nōbīs** to/for us
abl.	**mē** by me	**nōbīs** by us
nom.	**tū** you	**vōs** you
acc.	**tē** you	**vōs** you
gen.	**tuī** of you	**vestrī** of you
dat.	**tibi** to/for you	**vōbīs** to/for you
abl.	**tē** by you	**vōbīs** by you

nom.	—
acc.	**sē** himself, herself, themselves
gen.	**suī** of himself, herself, themselves
dat.	**sibi** to/for himself, herself, themselves
abl.	**sē** by himself, herself, themselves

NB

1 Modern English uses the same forms – 'you' – for singular and plural; Latin has separate forms.
2 **sē** has the same forms for singular and plural.
3 **sē** has no nominative since it is only used to refer back to the subject of the verb (see below).
4 **ego, tū, nōs, vōs** are used in the nominative only for emphasis, e.g.

> **ego labōrō, tū lūdis** I am working, you are playing.

> **nōs festīnāmus, vōs lentē ambulātis** We are hurrying, you are going slowly.

Personal pronouns can be used reflexively, i.e. referring back to the subject of the verb, e.g.

		(compare French:
ego mē lavō	I wash myself	*je me lave*
tū tē lavās	you wash yourself	*tu te laves*
ille sē lavat	he washes himself	*il se lave*
nōs nōs lavāmus	we wash ourselves	*nous nous lavons*
vōs vōs lavātis	you wash yourselves	*vous vous lavez*
illī sē lavant	they wash themselves	*ils se lavent)*

Note that although Latin says **mē lavō** ('I wash myself'), in English we can say simply 'I wash'. So also **Scintilla sē parat** ('Scintilla prepares herself'), but we usually say 'prepares', 'gets ready'. And **pater sē vertit** ('father turns himself'), where we usually say 'turns'.

In Latin such transitive verbs (i.e. verbs requiring an object) usually have the reflexive pronoun as the object where English can use the verb intransitively (i.e. without any object).

Exercise 14.2

Translate the following

1 Scintilla cēnam parat.
2 Horātia ad cēnam sē parat.
3 nautae nāvem ad lītus vertunt.
4 nautae sē vertunt et nōs salūtant.

5 puerī canem in viā exercent.
6 cūr in agrō vōs exercētis?
7 pater fīlium iubet sibi succurrere.
8 fēminae fīliās iubent sēcum ad fontem venīre.

Note the following personal adjectives:

meus, mea, meum	my	**noster, nostra, nostrum**	our
tuus, tua, tuum	your	**vester, vestra, vestrum**	your
suus, sua, suum*	his/her own	**suus, sua, suum***	their own

*reflexive, e.g.

> **Crassus cupit suam glōriam augēre** Crassus wants to increase his (own) glory.

> **puerī suōs loculōs ferunt** The boys are carrying their (own) satchels.

For non-reflexive 'his', e.g. the tutor is carrying his (= the boy's) satchel, **eius** (= of him) is used; **eōrum** (= of them) is used for 'their', e.g.:

> **puerī ad lūdum festīnant; paedagōgī loculōs eōrum ferunt.**
> The boys are hurrying to school; the tutors are carrying their satchels.

> **Quīntus domum currit; amīcus eius lentē ambulat.**
> Quintus runs home; his friend walks slowly.

> **MEMENTO**: Remember: 'his' in English could refer either to the subject of the sentence or to someone else; but Latin uses **suus** if it refers to the subject, **eius** if it refers to someone else.

Exercise 14.3

ego mē vertō = I turn round (literally: 'I turn myself'). *Translate*:

you (*singular*) turn round, he turns round, we turn round, you (*plural*) turn round, they turn round.

Exercise 14.4

Translate

1 Argus malus canis est; in lutō (*mud*) sē volvit (*rolls*) et valdē sordidus est.
2 Scintilla 'Argus' inquit 'valdē sordidus est; dēbētis eum lavāre.'
3 Quīntus 'ō canis sordide,' inquit, 'cūr nōn potes tē lavāre? ego nōn cupiō tē lavāre.'
4 Scintilla 'vōs parate, puerī,' inquit; 'dēbētis canem vestrum statim lavāre.'
5 Quīntus ad mātrem sē vertit et 'ego occupātus (*busy*) sum' inquit; 'Horātia ipsa (*herself*) suum canem lavāre dēbet.'
6 Horātia 'nōlī ignāvus (*lazy*) esse, Quīnte,' inquit; 'Argus nōn meus canis est sed tuus.'
7 tandem Quīntus urnam aquae fert Horātiamque iuvat. Argum diū lavant.
8 ubi prīmum canem solvunt (*untie*), ille abit iterumque in lūtō sē volvit.

Exercise 14.5

In the following sentences fill the blanks with the correct pronouns and translate, e.g.

> **ubi — vertimus, patrem vidēmus, quī ab agrō redit. (nōs)**
> When we turn round, we see father, who is returning from the field.

1 Scintilla ad Horātiam — vertit; 'parā — ad cēnam, Horātia,' inquit.
2 Horātia, quae — lavat, 'veniō statim,' inquit; 'iam — parō.'
3 Quīntus in agrō — exercet; arborem altam (*high*) ascendit.
4 subitō ad terram cadit; patrem iubet — succurrere.
5 mīlitēs in agrō sedent; centuriō 'cūr in agrō ōtiōsī (*idle*) sedētis, mīlitēs?' inquit; 'cūr nōn — exercētis?'
6 illī invītī surgunt et — exercent.

Chapter 15

The irregular verbs 'volō' and 'nōlō'

Learn these verbs: **volō** I wish, I am willing, and **nōlō** I am unwilling, I refuse:

volō	I wish	**nōlō**	I am unwilling
vīs	you wish	**nōn vīs**	you are unwilling
vult	he/she wishes	**nōn vult**	he/she is unwilling
volumus	we wish	**nōlumus**	we are unwilling
vultis	you wish	**nōn vultis**	you are unwilling
volunt	they wish	**nōlunt**	they are unwilling

infinitive	**velle**		**nōlle**
imperatives:	*singular*		**nōlī**
	plural		**nōlīte**

a negative command

Note that **volō** has no imperatives. **nōlī**, **nōlīte** are used in prohibitions, as we have seen (chapter 8).

Irregular imperatives

Note the following (the irregular forms are in bold type):

dīcō: **dīc**	dūcō: **dūc**	ferō: **fer**	facio: **fac**
dīcite	dūcite	**ferte**	facite

Exercise 15.1

Pick out from the English translations below the ones which fit the following verb forms

1	tollunt	4	adeunt	7	velle	10	dīc
2	esse	5	volumus	8	quiēscimus	11	possumus
3	canite	6	ferte	9	venīte	12	īte

13	nōlunt		
14	posse		
15	stāmus		

to be, we are resting, we stand, they lift, bring!, sing!, say!, to wish, we can,
they approach, come!, they refuse, we are willing, go!, to be able

Demonstrative pronouns

Learn the following pronouns (for their declension compare **is** and **ille** in chapter 14):

hic, haec, hoc this (here)

	singular			*plural*		
	m.	*f.*	*n.*	*m.*	*f.*	*n.*
nom.	hic	haec	hoc	hī	hae	haec
acc.	hunc	hanc	hoc	hōs	hās	haec
gen.	huius	huius	huius	hōrum	hārum	hōrum
dat.	huic	huic	huic	hīs	hīs	hīs
abl.	hōc	hāc	hōc	hīs	hīs	hīs

he   she   it

(this rather   than   that)

ipse, ipsa, ipsum self (emphasizing, e.g. **Flaccus ipse** Flaccus himself; **Horātia ipsa** Horatia herself; **eō ipsō tempore** at that very time)

	singular			*plural*		
	m.	*f.*	*n.*	*m.*	*f.*	*n.*
nom.	ipse	ipsa	ipsum	ipsī	ipsae	ipsa
acc.	ipsum	ipsam	ipsum	ipsōs	ipsās	ipsa
gen.	ipsīus	ipsīus	ipsīus	ipsōrum	ipsārum	ipsōrum
dat.	ipsī	ipsī	ipsī	ipsīs	ipsīs	ipsīs
abl.	ipsō	ipsā	ipsō	ipsīs	ipsīs	ipsīs

Exercise 15.2

Translate

1 Mercurius ipse Aenēam iubet ad Italiam nāvigāre.
2 ille hoc facere nōn vult.
3 sed nōn potest deōrum ipsōrum imperia neglegere.
4 ad comitēs festīnat eōsque iubet nāvēs parāre.
5 illō ipsō diē Dīdō haec cognōscit.
6 ipsa Aenēam arcessit eumque rogat dē hīs.
7 Aenēās eī haec respondet: 'Iuppiter ipse mē iubet Italiam petere.'
8 ubi Trōiānī ā Libyā nāvigant, Dīdō ipsa suā manū sē occīdit.

Exercise 15.3

Decline the following phrases in all cases (except vocative)

in the singular	*in the plural*
magnum mare	ingentia saxa
haec puella	marītī trīstēs
pater ipse	illī senēs

Exercise 15.4

Translate

1 hostēs nōs circumveniunt; nōlumus hīc manēre; dēbēmus ē castrīs ērumpere (*break out*).
2 cōnsul ipse hostēs timet nec vult exercitum in eōs dūcere.
3 nēmō nōs servāre potest nisi (*except*) Cincinnātus ipse. itaque arcessite eum ad urbem.
4 'Cincinnāte, hunc exercitum in hostēs dūc et auxilium fer ad cōnsulis legiōnēs.'
5 Cincinnātus exercitum in hostēs dūcit; hostēs in proeliō vincit servatque et cōnsulem ipsum et legiōnēs eius.

Exercise 15.5

Translate into Latin

1 After supper Flaccus is often willing to tell stories to the children.
2 Quintus always wants to hear stories about wars and soldiers.
3 These stories please Flaccus himself, who tells them well.

4 Horatia does not want to hear these things; both Scintilla and she herself want to hear stories about Roman women.

5 When Flaccus and Quintus are not there, Scintilla sometimes (**nōnnumquam**) tells stories about women.

6 Horatia listens to these stories happily.

Appendix   Ciceronis filius

The following passage gives a short account of the early years of the young Marcus Cicero, only son of the great orator and statesman. Unlike Quintus, who is the son of a freedman, a small-time farmer living in a remote country town in Apulia, Marcus Cicero is the son of one of the leading statesmen of the time, attended by an army of slaves and surrounded by a continual bustle of political activity. The contrast between his way of life and that of Quintus in his early years could scarcely be greater.

In our main story, when Quintus is taken by his father to Rome to attend the school of Orbilius, he is befriended by Marcus, who is also studying there. This friendship is fictional, though it is possible that they met in Athens or later in the army of Brutus; both served at the battle of Philippi. Our story ends abruptly with the meeting of Marcus and Quintus; it will be taken up again in Part II, chapter 20.

Cicerō epistolās dictat scrībae suō Tīrōnī. subitō aliquis iānuam pulsat. incurrit servus. 'domine,' inquit, 'nūntium valdē bonum tibi ferō. Terentia fīliolum peperit. et māter et īnfāns valent.' Cicerō 're vērā' inquit 'nūntium bonum mihi portās. Tīrō,
5 servōs iubē equōs parāre. dēbēmus ad Terentiam festīnāre.'

mox equī parātī sunt. Cicerō Tīrōque Rōmā statim abeunt Arpīnumque festīnant. postrīdiē ad vīllam adveniunt. Tullia, Cicerōnis fīlia, quae iam decem annōs nāta est, adventum eōrum audit. ad iānuam currit patremque salūtat. 'venī, pater,' inquit;
10 'festīnā. īnfāns valdē pulcher est.' patrem in tablīnum dūcit. ibi in lectō iacet Terentia, pallida sed laeta; prope lectum sunt cūnae, in quibus dormit parvus īnfāns.

Cicerō ad uxōrem accēdit et ōsculum eī dat. 'uxor cāra,' inquit, 'quid agis?' īnfantem spectat. 'quam pulcher est īnfāns!' inquit;
15 'quam laetus sum quod tū valēs.' sīc dīcit īnfantemque ē cūnīs

epistolās letters; **scrībae** to his secretary; **aliquis** someone
servus a slave; **domine** master!
fīliolum peperit has given birth to a little son; **valent** are well
re vērā in truth
Arpīnum to Arpinum
vīllam (country) house
decem annōs nāta est is ten years old
adventum arrival
tablīnum reception room
lectō a bed; **pallida** pale
sunt cūnae there is a cradle
in quibus in which
ōsculum kiss
quid agis? how are you?

tollit; fīliolō arrīdet; 'salvē, fīliole,' inquit; 'salvē, Marce; nam sīc
tē nōminō.' īnfantem ancillae trādit sedetque prope Terentiam.
aliquamdiū cum uxōre manet. tandem 'fessa es, cārissima,'
inquit; 'dormīre dēbēs.' ancilla īnfantem ē tablīnō portat; quattuor
20   servī Terentiam in lectō ad cubiculum portant.

arrīdet (+ dat.) he smiles at
salvē greetings!; nōminō I name
ancillae to a servant girl
aliquamdiū for some time
cubiculum bedroom

postrīdiē Cicerō Rōmam redit; nam cōnsulātum petit et multīs
negōtiīs occupātus est. parvō Marcō ōsculum dat; uxōrem
fīliamque valēre iubet. deinde cum Tīrōne ex aulā equitat.

cōnsulātum the consulship
negōtiīs business(es)
valēre iubet (+ acc.) says goodbye to
aulā the courtyard; equitat rides

dum parvus est, Marcus plērumque in vīllā habitat. māter
25   paterque saepe absunt; nam pater vir īnsignis est quī, ubi Marcus
duōs annōs nātus est, cōnsul fit. nūtrīx eum cūrat, et Tullia, quae
frātrem valdē amat, plērumque adest. vīlla satis ampla est sed
nōn splendida, in collibus Sabīnīs sita. pater Marcī saepe eō redit
cum rēbus pūblicīs nōn occupātus est; nam semper cupit fīliolum
30   vidēre gaudetque domum suam redīre. Cicerōnis frāter, Quīntus
Cicerō, ad vīllam saepe venit cum uxōre Pompōniā fīliōque
Quīntō. Marcus laetus est cum Quīntus adest; Quīntum enim
amat diūque cum eō lūdit.

plērumque usually
absunt are absent, away
īnsignis important
cōnsul fit becomes, is made consul
   (63 BC); nūtrīx nurse
satis ampla large enough
sita sited, positioned
rēbus pūblicīs with public affairs

Marcus quīntum annum agit cum pater cōnstituit eum ad
35   urbem Rōmam dūcere. ibi in aedibus magnificīs habitat in monte
Palātīnō sitīs. aedēs semper hominibus plēnae sunt. multī servī
ancillaeque discurrunt officiīs fungentēs. multī clientēs ad aedēs
māne veniunt patremque salūtant. senātōrēs ad patrem veniunt
cōnsiliumque eius rogant. pater plērumque negōtiīs occupātus
40   est; longās epistolās scrībae dictat; saepe ad senātum īre dēbet
diūque abest dum senātōrēs rēs pūblicās disserunt. māter quoque
semper occupāta est; nam domina familiae est; omnēs servōs
omnēsque ancillās regit; et mātrōnās nōbilēs saepe accipit quae
ad aedēs veniunt eamque salūtant.

cum when
aedibus (f. pl.) house
plēnae (+ abl.) full of
discurrunt are running about
officiīs fungentēs performing their
   duties; māne in the morning
cōnsilium advice
disserunt discuss
domina familiae mistress of the
   household; mātrōnās ladies

45   Marcum iam cūrat nōn nūtrīx sed paedagōgus Graecus. ille
Marcum litterās docet et Latīnās et Graecās; plērumque Marcō
Graecē dīcit. ille studia nōn amat; nam semper lūdere cupit. sed
Graecē et dīcere et scrībere gradātim discit.

paedagōgus tutor

Graecē in Greek; studia his studies
gradātim little by little; discit learns

ubi venit aestās, tōta familia ab urbe in collēs abit ad vīllam
50   rūsticam; nam calōrēs aestātis in urbe ferre nōn possunt. ibi
Marcus fēriās agit. cōnsōbrīnus eius Quīntus ad vīllam saepe
venit. puerī in agrīs lūdunt, fundum vīsunt, piscēs in flūmine
capiunt. cum autumnus adest, in urbem redeunt. hīs fēriīs Marcus
valdē gaudet.

aestās summer
calōrēs the heat(s)
fēriās agit is on holiday
cōnsōbrīnus eius his cousin
fundum the farm; vīsunt visit
piscēs fish

55   ubi Marcus septimum annum agit, inimīcī lēgem in
Cicerōnem ferunt. ille inimīcōs valdē timet cōnstituitque in
exsilium fugere. Terentiam iubet Rōmā abīre et in vīllā rūsticā

inimīcī enemies;
lēgem ferunt pass (bring) a law
in against

manēre. trīstis Rōmā discēdit et ad Graeciam nāvigat. Terentia
tōtam familiam ad vīllam dūcit ibique manet dum Cicerō abest.
60 Marcus patrem dēsīderat sed gaudet quod fēriās tam longās agit.
intereā Cicerō epistolās miserās ad Terentiam scrībit semperque
cupit Rōmam redīre. sed proximō annō amīcī eius novam lēgem
ferunt eumque ex exsiliō revocant.

Cicerō, ubi Rōmam redit, familiam ad urbem revocat. dum
65 abest, aedēs eius ab inimīcīs dēlētae sunt sed Cicerō novās aedēs
celeriter aedificat, magnās et splendidās. Marcus trīstis est quod
rūre discēdere dēbet sed laetus quod pater adest. nunc pater ipse
studia eius cūrat; Marcus dēbet multō dīligentius studēre.

paucīs post annīs, ubi Marcus quattuordecim annōs nātus est,
70 senātōrēs Cicerōnem ad Ciliciam mittunt ut prōvinciam
administret. Cicerō invītus Rōmā discēdit sed cōnstituit Marcum
sēcum dūcere. iter longum et labōriōsum perficere dēbent.
prīmum in Graeciam nāvigant et diū Athēnīs manent; Marcus
omnia monumenta vīsit novōsque amīcōs facit inter puerōs
75 Graecōs.

deinde terrā iter faciunt. lentē prōcēdunt et in viā clārās urbēs
Asiae vīsunt. ubi tandem in Ciliciam adveniunt, prōvincia in
magnō perīculō est, quod hostēs fīnēs oppugnant. Cicerō bellum
in eōs īnferre dēbet. ubi hostibus occurrit, Marcus proelium
80 spectāre cupit, sed pater eum iubet in castrīs manēre. Cicerō
hostēs vincit expellitque ē prōvinciā.

proximō annō Cicerō ā Ciliciā discēdit Marcumque domum
redūcit. ubi Rōmam redeunt, bellum cīvīle reīpūblicae imminet.
Cicerō valdē occupātus est néc fīliī studia cūrāre potest. itaque
85 Marcum ad lūdum Orbiliī mittit. Marcus invītus studet; iam
iuvenis est cupitque ā lūdō discēdere. sed multōs amīcōs facit;
inter aliōs iuvenī cuidam occurrit nōmine Quīntō Horātiō Flaccō,
quī Rōmam ab Apūliā nūper advēnit. ille modestus est et facētus;
Marcus eum dīligit patrīque commendat. Cicerō gaudet quod
90 fīlius eius amīcum tam modestum tamque industrium habet; nam
Quīntus studiīs gaudet et dīligenter labōrat; sed Marcus semper
cupit cum iuvenibus lautīs lūdere et saepe nimium vīnī cum eīs
bibit.

---

discēdit goes away from, leaves

dēsīderat misses

proximō annō the next year

ab inimīcīs by his enemies
dēlētae sunt has been destroyed
rūre from the country
multō dīligentius much harder

paucīs post annīs a few years later
quattuordecim annōs nātus
  fourteen years old
ut prōvinciam administret to
  govern the province
invītus reluctant(ly); **iter** journey
Athēnīs at Athens

terrā by land; **clārās** famous

fīnēs the boundaries
īnferre to wage

bellum cīvīle civil war
reīpūblicae the republic
imminet (+ dat.) threatens

cuidam (dat.) a certain
nūper advēnit who arrived recently
facētus witty; **dīligit** likes
commendat introduces
tam modestum so modest
lautīs smart; **nimium vīnī** too
  much wine

Reference grammar

NOUNS

	1st declension	2nd declension			
	stems in **-a**	stems in **-o**			
	feminine	*masculine*			*neuter*
singular					
nom.	puell-a	colōn-us	puer	ager	bell-um
voc.	puell-a	colōn-e	puer	ager	bell-um
acc.	puell-am	colōn-um	puer-um	agr-um	bell-um
gen.	puell-ae	colōn-ī	puer-ī	agr-ī	bell-ī
dat.	puell-ae	colōn-ō	puer-ō	agr-ō	bell-ō
abl.	puell-ā	colōn-ō	puer-ō	agr-ō	bell-ō
plural					
nom.	puell-ae	colōn-ī	puer-ī	agr-ī	bell-a
voc.	puell-ae	colōn-ī	puer-ī	agr-ī	bell-a
acc.	puell-ās	colōn-ōs	puer-ōs	agr-ōs	bell-a
gen.	puell-ārum	colōn-ōrum	puer-ōrum	agr-ōrum	bell-ōrum
dat.	puell-īs	colōn-īs	puer-īs	agr-īs	bell-īs
abl.	puell-īs	colōn-īs	puer-īs	agr-īs	bell-īs

Notes

1 All nouns of the 1st declension are feminine except for a very few which are masculine by meaning, e.g. **nauta** a sailor.

2 The vocative is the same as the nominative except for the vocative singular of 2nd declension nouns with nominative **-us**, e.g. **colōn-e**.

The vocative of 2nd declension nouns with nominative **-ius** ends **-ī**, not **-e**, e.g. **fīlī**.

	3rd declension			
	stems in consonants		stems in **-i**	
	masc. & fem.	*neuter*	*masc. & fem.*	*neuter*
singular				
nom.	rēx	lītus	nāvis	mare
acc.	rēg-em	lītus	nāv-em	mare
gen.	rēg-is	lītor-is	nāv-is	mar-is
dat.	rēg-ī	lītor-ī	nāv-ī	mar-ī
abl.	rēg-e	lītor-e	nāv-e	mar-ī
plural				
nom.	rēg-ēs	lītor-a	nāv-ēs	mar-ia
acc.	rēg-ēs	lītor-a	nāv-ēs	mar-ia
gen.	rēg-um	lītor-um	nāv-ium	mar-ium
dat.	rēg-ibus	lītor-ibus	nāv-ibus	mar-ibus
abl.	rēg-ibus	lītor-ibus	nāv-ibus	mar-ibus

Notes

1 The vocative case is the same as the nominative in all 3rd declension nouns and adjectives.

2 Masculine and feminine nouns with stems in **-i** nearly all decline like those with stems in consonants except in the genitive plural, where the **-i** is retained, e.g. **nāvium**; neuter nouns with stems in **-i** keep the **-i** in ablative singular, and the nominative, accusative and genitive plural (see **mare** above).

Nouns ending in two consonants (the second **-s**), e.g. **mōns**, **urbs** (originally spelt **monis**, **urbis**) have genitive plural **-ium**.

3 **iuvenis**, **senex** and **canis** have genitive plural **-um**.

4 A few 3rd declension nouns can, by sense, be either masculine or feminine in gender, e.g. **comes**, **comitis** a companion; these are marked *c.* (= common) in vocabulary lists.

ADJECTIVES

Masculine & neuter 2nd declension; feminine 1st declension

singular	m. *bonus*	f. *puella*	n. *bellum*
nom.	bon-us	bon-a	bon-um
voc.	bon-e	bon-a	bon-um
acc.	bon-um	bon-am	bon-um
gen.	bon-ī	bon-ae	bon-ī
dat.	bon-ō	bon-ae	bon-ō
abl.	bon-ō	bon-ā	bon-ō

plural			
nom.	bon-ī	bon-ae	bon-a
voc.	bon-ī	bon-ae	bon-a
acc.	bon-ōs	bon-ās	bon-a
gen.	bon-ōrum	bon-ārum	bon-ōrum
dat.	bon-īs	bon-īs	bon-īs
abl.	bon-īs	bon-īs	bon-īs

So also:

miser, miser-a, miser-um, etc.,
pulcher, pulchr-a, pulchr-um, etc.

For **miser** and **pulcher** types of adjective the vocative is the same as the nominative.

3rd declension

	consonant stems		stems in **-i**	
singular	m. & f.	n.	m. & f.	n.
nom.	pauper	pauper	omnis	omn-e
acc.	pauper-em	pauper	omn-em	omn-e
gen.	pauper-is	pauper-is	omn-is	omn-is
dat.	pauper-ī	pauper-ī	omn-ī	omn-ī
abl.	pauper-e	pauper-e	omn-ī	omn-ī

plural				
nom.	pauper-ēs	pauper-a	omn-ēs	omn-ia
acc.	pauper-ēs	pauper-a	omn-ēs	omn-ia
gen.	pauper-um	pauper-um	omn-ium	omn-ium
dat.	pauper-ibus	pauper-ibus	omn-ibus	omn-ibus
abl.	pauper-ibus	pauper-ibus	omn-ibus	omn-ibus

Notes

1 The vocative is the same as the nominative.
2 Most 3rd declension adjectives have stems in **-i**; these keep the **-i** in ablative singular, genitive plural, and in neuter nominative and accusative plural.
3 Other types of 3rd declension adjectives with stems in **-i** are:

	m. & f.	n.
nom.	ingēns	ingēns
gen.	ingentis	ingentis
nom.	fēlīx	fēlīx
gen.	fēlīcis	fēlīcis

ADVERBS

1 From **bonus** type adjectives, adverbs are usually formed by adding **-ē** to the stem, e.g. **lent-us** slow: **lent-ē** slowly; **miser** miserable: **miser-ē** miserably. A few add **-ō**, e.g. **subit-us** sudden: **subit-ō** suddenly.
Note **bonus, -a, -um** forms adverb **bene**.

2 From 3rd declension adjectives, adverbs are usually formed by adding **-ter** to the stem, e.g. **fēlīx** fortunate: **fēlīci-ter** fortunately; **celer** quick: **celeri-ter** quickly.

3 There are many adverbs which have no corresponding adjectival form, e.g. **diū, quandō? iam, semper**.

NUMERALS

1	ūnus
2	duo
3	trēs
4	quattuor
5	quīnque
6	sex
7	septem
8	octō
9	novem
10	decem

The numbers 4–10 do not decline.

Declension of ūnus, duo, trēs

	m.	f.	n.	m.	f.	n.	m.	f.	n.
nom.	ūnus	ūna	ūnum	duo	duae	duo	trēs	trēs	tria
acc.	ūnum	ūnam	ūnum	duōs	duās	duo	trēs	trēs	tria
gen.	ūnīus	ūnīus	ūnīus	duōrum	duārum	duōrum	trium	trium	trium
dat.	ūnī	ūnī	ūnī	duōbus	duābus	duōbus	tribus	tribus	tribus
abl.	ūnō	ūnā	ūnō	duōbus	duābus	duōbus	tribus	tribus	tribus

PREPOSITIONS

The following take the accusative:

ad	to, towards
ante	before
circum	around
extrā	outside
in	into, onto
inter	among
per	through
post	after, behind
prope	near
trāns	across

The following take the ablative:

ā/ab	from
cum	with
dē	down from; about
ē/ex	out of
in	in, on
sine	without
sub	under

PRONOUNS

singular

nom.	ego (I)	tū (you)	
acc.	mē	tē	sē (himself, herself)
gen.	meī	tuī	suī
dat.	mihi	tibi	sibi
abl.	mē	tē	sē

Possessive adjectives:

meus, -a, -um (my)
tuus, -a, -um (your)
suus, -a, -um (his own)

plural

nom.	nōs (we)	vōs (you)	
acc.	nōs	vōs	sē (themselves)
gen.	nostrum, nostrī	vestrum, vestrī	suī
dat.	nōbīs	vōbīs	sibi
abl.	nōbīs	vōbīs	sē

noster, nostra, nostrum (our)
vester, vestra, vestrum (your)
suus, -a, -um (their own)
All decline like **bonus, -a, -um**,
but the vocative of **meus** is **mī**

singular

	m.	f.	n.	m.	f.	n.	m.	f.	n.
nom.	hic	haec	hoc (this)	ille	illa	illud (that)	is	ea	id (he, she, it)
acc.	hunc	hanc	hoc	illum	illam	illud	eum	eam	id
gen.	huius	huius	huius	illīus	illīus	illīus	eius	eius	eius
dat.	huic	huic	huic	illī	illī	illī	eī	eī	eī
abl.	hōc	hāc	hōc	illō	illā	illō	eō	eā	eō

plural

	m.	f.	n.	m.	f.	n.	m.	f.	n.
nom.	hī	hae	haec	illī	illae	illa	eī	eae	ea
acc.	hōs	hās	haec	illōs	illās	illa	eōs	eās	ea
gen.	hōrum	hārum	hōrum	illōrum	illārum	illōrum	eōrum	eārum	eōrum
dat.	hīs	hīs	hīs	illīs	illīs	illīs	eīs	eīs	eīs
abl.	hīs	hīs	hīs	illīs	illīs	illīs	eīs	eīs	eīs

singular

	m.	f.	n.	m.	f.	n.
nom.	ipse	ipsa	ipsum (self)	quī	quae	quod (who, which)
acc.	ipsum	ipsam	ipsum	quem	quam	quod
gen.	ipsīus	ipsīus	ipsīus	cuius	cuius	cuius
dat.	ipsī	ipsī	ipsī	cui	cui	cui
abl.	ipsō	ipsā	ipsō	quō	quā	quō

plural

	m.	f.	n.	m.	f.	n.
nom.	ipsī	ipsae	ipsa	quī	quae	quae
acc.	ipsōs	ipsas	ipsa	quōs	quās	quae
gen.	ipsōrum	ipsārum	ipsōrum	quōrum	quārum	quōrum
dat.	ipsīs	ipsīs	ipsīs	quibus	quibus	quibus
abl.	ipsīs	ipsīs	ipsīs	quibus	quibus	quibus

VERBS

	1st conj.	*2nd conj.*	*3rd conj.*	*4th conj.*	*mixed conj.*
	stems in -**a**	stems in -**e**	stems in consonants	stems in -**i**	
sing.	par-ō	mone-ō	reg-ō	audi-ō	capi-ō
	parā-s	monē-s	reg-is	audī-s	cap-is
	para-t	mone-t	reg-it	audi-t	cap-it
plur.	parā-mus	monē-mus	reg-imus	audī-mus	cap-imus
	parā-tis	monē-tis	reg-itis	audī-tis	cap-itis
	para-nt	mone-nt	reg-unt	audi-unt	capi-unt

infinitive					
	parā-re	monē-re	reg-ere	audī-re	cap-ere

imperatives					
sing.	parā	monē	reg-e	audī	cap-e
plur.	parā-te	monē-te	reg-ite	audī-te	cap-ite

Irregular Verbs

	sum	**possum** (**pot + sum**)	**eō** (stem **i-**)	**volō**	**nōlō**
sing.	sum	pos-sum	eō	volō	nōlō
	e-s	pot-es	ī-s	vīs	nōn vīs
	es-t	pot-est	i-t	vult	nōn vult
plur.	su-mus	pos-sumus	ī-mus	volumus	nōlumus
	es-tis	pot-estis	ī-tis	vultis	nōn vultis
	su-nt	pos-sunt	e-unt	volunt	nōlunt

infinitive					
	esse	posse	ī-re	velle	nōlle

imperatives					
sing.	es, es-tō	-	ī	-	nōlī
plur.	es-te	-	ī-te	-	nōlīte

CONJUNCTIONS

Coordinating

et	and
et ... et	both ... and
sed	but
nam	for
nec/neque	and not, nor
nec/neque ... nec/neque	neither ... nor
aut	or
aut ... aut	either ... or
itaque	and so

Subordinating

ubi	when
quod	because
dum	while
sī	if
(**cum**	when)

Vocabulary

Latin – English

The numbers after the words give the chapter vocabularies in which the words occur; those with no number have not been learned. Words which are glossed and which do not recur are omitted from this list.

ā/ab + abl. (7) from
abeō, abīre I go away
abhinc ago
accēdō, accēdere (4) I approach
accendō, accendere I set on fire
accipiō, accipere (9) I receive, accept
accūsō, accūsāre I accuse
Achillēs, Achillis, *m.* Achilles
ad + acc. (3) to, towards
admīrātiō, admīrātiōnis, *f.* wonder, admiration
adsum, adesse (4) I am present
adveniō, advenīre (5) I arrive
aedes, aedium, *f. pl.* house
aedificō, aedificāre (11) I build
age! come on!
ager, agrī, *m.* (3) field
agō, agere I drive, I do
alius, alia, aliud (5) other
    aliī ... aliī some ... others
ambulō, ambulāre (1) I walk
amīcus, -ī, *m.* (4) friend
amō, amāre (12) I love
amor, amōris, *m.* (12) love
animus, -ī, *m.* (12) mind
ante + acc. (12) before
anteā (adv.) before
ānxius, -a, -um (3) anxious
aqua, aquae, *f.* (2) water
arbor, arboris, *f.* (13) tree
arma, armōrum, *n. pl.* (11) arms, weapons
arx, arcis, *f.* citadel
ascendō, ascendere (3) I climb
asinus, -ī, *m.* ass
attendō, attendere I attend
attonitus, -a, -um astonished
audiō, audīre (3) I hear
aura, -ae, *f.* (13) breeze, air
aut ... aut (12) either ... or
auxilium, -ī, *n.* (15) help

bellum, -ī, *n.* (11) war
bellum gerō, gerere (15) I wage war
bene (8) well
benignus, -a, -um kind
bibō, bibere (9) I drink
bonus, -a, -um (5) good

cadō, cadere (3) I fall
caelum, -ī, *n.* (10) sky, heaven
canis, canis, *c.* (7) dog
canō, canere (14) I sing
capiō, capere (7) I take
capsula, -ae, *f.* satchel
carmen, carminis, *n.* (14) song
cārus, -a, -um (7) dear
casa, -ae, *f.* (1) house, cottage
castra, castrōrum, *n. pl.* (11) camp
caveō, cavēre I beware, I watch out
celer, celeris, celere quick
celeriter (6) quickly
cēna, -ae, *f.* (1) dinner
cēnō, cēnāre (1) I dine
centuriō, centuriōnis, *m.* (14) centurion
cessō, cessāre I linger, idle
cēterī, cēterae, cētera (6) the others, the rest
cibus, -ī, *m.* (3) food
circum + acc. (8) around
circumveniō, circumvenīre (15) I surround
cīvis, cīvis, *c.* (15) citizen
clāmō, clāmāre (5) I shout
clāmor, clāmōris, *m.* (10) shout
clārus, -a, -um bright, clear, famous
cliēns, clientis, *m.* client
cognōscō, cognōscere (11) I get to know, learn
collis, collis, *m.* (11) hill
colloquium, -ī, *n.* conversation, talk
colō, colere (13) I till; I worship
colōnia, -ae, *f.* colony
colōnus, -ī, *m.* (3) farmer
comes, comitis, *c.* (7) comrade
commōtus, -a, -um (12) moved
condō, condere I found
cōnfectus, -a, -um finished
coniciō, conicere (8) I hurl
cōnscendō, cōnscendere (9) I board (a ship)
cōnsilium, -ī, *n.* (11) plan
cōnsistō, cōnsistere I halt, stop
cōnsōlātiō, cōnsōlātiōnis, *f.* consolation, comfort
cōnstituō, cōnstituere (6) I decide
cōnsul, cōnsulis, *m.* (15) consul
cōnsūmō, cōnsūmere I consume, eat
contendō, contendere (14) I walk, march, hasten
contingō, contingere I touch, reach
conveniō, convenīre (9) I come together, meet
convocō, convocāre (7) I call together
cotīdiē every day
crās tomorrow
cum + abl. (5) with
cum (conjunction) when

Cupīdō, Cupīdinis, *m.* Cupid
cupiō, cupere (6) I desire, want
cūr? (4) why?
cūrō, cūrāre (4) I care for, look after
currō, currere (3) I run
custōdiō, custōdīre (16) I guard
custōs, custōdis, *m.* (16) guard
Cyclōps, Cyclōpis, *m.* a Cyclops

dē + abl. (10) down from
dē + abl. (15) about
dea, deae, *f.* (12) goddess
dēbeō, dēbēre (6) I ought, I must
dēcurrō, dēcurrere I run down
dēdō, dēdere (15) I give up, surrender
dēdūcō, dēdūcere I lead down
dēfendō, dēfendere (7) I defend
deinde then, next
dēnārius, -ī, *m.* a penny
dēpōnō, dēpōnere (13) I put down
dēscendō, dēscendere I descend
dēserō, dēserere I desert
dēsertus, -a, -um deserted
dēsistō, dēsistere I cease from
dēspērō, dēspērāre (12) I despair
deus, deī, *m.* (12) a god
dēvorō, dēvorāre I swallow down, devour
dī immortālēs! immortal gods!
dīcō, dīcere (5) I say
dictātor, dictātōris, *m.* (15) dictator
dictō, dictāre I dictate
Dīdō, Dīdōnis, *f.* Dido
diēs, diēī, *m.* day
dignus, -a, -um (+ abl.) (16) worthy (of)
dīligēns, dīligentis careful, diligent
dīligenter (6) carefully, hard
dīmittō, dīmittere (6) I send away, dismiss
discō, discere I learn
diū (4) for a long time
diūtius for a longer time, longer
dīvīnus, -a, -um (13) divine
dō, dare (5) I give
doceō, docēre (6) I teach
domina, -ae, *f.* (13) mistress
domum (6) (to) home
domus, -ī, *f.* (6) home
dōnum, -ī, *n.* gift
dormiō, dormīre (4) I sleep
dubius, -a, -um doubtful
   sine dubiō without doubt
dūcō, dūcere (3) I lead; draw (water)
dum (11) while
duo, duae, duo (5) two

eam, eum (3) (acc. sing.) her, him
eās, eōs (acc. pl.) them
ecce! look!

ē/ex + abl. (8) out of, from
edō, edere I eat
effugiō, effugere I flee from, escape
ego (6) I (acc. **mē**)
ēmittō, ēmittere I send out
emō, emere (5) I buy
eō, īre (6) I go
eō (adv.) (14) (to) there, thither
eōs, eās (4) (acc. pl.) them
equus, equī, *m.* (9) horse
errō, errāre (11) I wander; I err, am wrong
ērumpō, ērumpere I break out
et (1) and
   et ... et (15) both ... and
etiam (12) even, also
ēvādō, ēvādere (16) I escape
ēvigilō, ēvigilāre (13) I wake up
excitō, excitāre (13) I rouse, awaken
exemplum, -ī, *n.* (16) example
exeō, exīre (6) I go out
exerceō, exercēre (14) I train, exercise
exercitus, -ūs, *m.* army
expellō, expellere I drive out
explōrō, explōrāre I explore
expōnō, expōnere I put out, explain
exsilium, -i, *n.* exile
exspectō, exspectāre (8) I wait for

fābula, -ae, *f.* (2) story; play
fābulōsus, -a, -um fabulous, from a story
facio, facere (5) I make; I do
fāma, -ae, *f.* (11) fame, report, reputation
familia, -ae, *f.* (14) family, household
fēlīx, fēlīcis (12) lucky, happy
fēmina, -ae, *f.* (1) woman
ferō, ferre (11) I carry, bear
fessus, -a, -um (1) tired
festīnō, festīnāre (1) I hurry
fīlia, -ae, *f.* (2) daughter
fīlius, -ī, *m.* (3) son
flamma, -ae, *f.* flame
flōs, flōris, *m.* (14) flower
flūmen, flūminis, *n.* (16) river
foedus, foederis, *n.* (16) treaty
fōns, fontis, *m.* spring
fōrma, -ae, *f.* (13) shape, beauty
fortis, forte (7) brave
fortiter (7) bravely
forum, -ī, *n.* city center, market place
frāter, frātris, *m.* (7) brother
frūmentum, -ī, *n.* (16) grain
fugiō, fugere (7) I flee
fūmus, -ī, *m.* smoke

gaudeō, gaudēre (9) I rejoice
gerō, gerere (14) I carry; I wear
gigas, gigantis, *m.* giant

glōria, -ae, *f.* (14) glory
Graecī, -ōrum, *m. pl.* Greeks
grātiae, -ārum, *f. pl.* thanks

habeō, habēre (9) I have
habitō, habitāre (10) I live, inhabit
hasta, -ae, *f.* (8) spear
haud (15) not
Hector, Hectoris, *m.* Hector
hīc (8) here
hic, haec, hoc (15) this
hiems, hiemis, *f.* (12) winter
hodiē (14) today
homō, hominis, *c.* (10) man, human being
horribilis, horribile horrible
hortus, -ī, *m.* (5) garden
hostis, hostis, *m.* (11) enemy
hūc (8) hither, (to) here

iaceō, iacēre (5) I lie (down)
iaciō, iacere (7) I throw
iam (4) now, already
iānua, -ae, *f.* (6) door
ibi (12) there
ignāvus, -a, -um lazy
ignōtus, -a, -um (11) unknown
ille, illa, illud (4) that; he, she, it
immemor, immemoris forgetful of
immittō, immittere I send into, send against
immortālis, immortāle immortal
imperātor, imperātōris, *m.* (14) general
imperium, -ī, *n.* (12) order
imperō, imperāre + dat. (11) I order
importō, importāre I carry into, import
impudēns, impudentis shameless, impudent
in + acc. (2) into, to
in + abl. (5) in, on
incipiō, incipere I begin
incolumis, incolume (8) unharmed, safe
īnfēlīx, īnfēlīcis (12) unlucky, ill-starred
ingēns, ingentis (9) huge
inquit (3) he/she says
    inquiunt they say
īnsula, -ae, *f.* (9) island
inter + acc. (9) among, between
intereā (12) meanwhile
intrō, intrāre (1) I enter
inveniō, invenīre (11) I find
invideō, invidēre + dat. (13) I envy
invītus, -a, -um unwilling
ipse, ipsa, ipsum (15) self
īra, -ae, *f.* (7) anger
īrātus, -a, -um (2) angry
is, ea, id (14) he, she, it; that
itaque (6) and so, therefore
iterum (6) again
iubeō, iubēre (6) I order

Iuppiter, Iovis, *m.* Jupiter
iuvenis, iuvenis, *m.* (14) young man
iuvō, iuvāre (2) I help

labor, labōris, *m.* (9) work, suffering
labōrō, labōrāre (1) I work
laetus, -a, -um (1) happy, joyful
laudō, laudāre (2) I praise
lavō, lavāre (14) I wash
legiō, legiōnis, *f.* (14) legion
lentē (4) slowly
līber, lībera, līberum (16) free
līberō, līberāre (16) I free
littera, -ae, *f.* (6) letter
lītus, lītoris, *n.* (10) shore
locus, -ī, *m.* (14) place
longus, -a, -um long
lūdō, lūdere (6) I play
lūdus, -ī, *m.* (4) school
lūgeō, lūgēre I mourn
lūx, lūcis, *f.* (13) light

magister, magistrī, *m.* (6) master
magnificē magnificently
magnus, -a, -um (4) great, big
malus, -a, -um (5) bad
maneō, manēre (3) I wait, await, stay, remain
manus, manūs, *f.* hand
mare, maris, *n.* (10) sea
marītus, -ī, *m.* (13) husband
māter, mātris, *f.* (8) mother
mē (acc.) (6) me
meus, -a, -um (6) my
mihi (dat.) to, for me
mīles, mīlitis, *m.* (14) soldier
miser, misera, miserum (4) miserable
mittō, mittere (3) I send
modestus, -a, -um modest
moenia, moenium, *n. pl.* (15) walls
moneō, monēre (9) I warn, advise
mōns, montis, *m.* (10) mountain
mōnstrum, -i, *n.* monster
monumentum, -ī, *n.* monument
mors, mortis, *f.* (8) death
mortuus, -a, -um (8) dead
mox (1) soon
multus, -a, -um (4) much, many
mūrus, -ī, *m.* (8) wall
Mycēnae, -ārum, *f. pl.* Mycenae

nam (3) for
nārrō, nārrāre (2) I tell, relate
nauta, -ae, *m.* (10) sailor
nāvigō, nāvigāre (7) I sail
nāvis, nāvis, *f.* (7) ship
nec/neque (5) nor, and not
    nec/neque ... nec/neque (6) neither ... nor

neglegō, neglegere I neglect
nēmō, nēminis, *c.* (13) no one
nimium, -ī, *n.* (5) too much
nisi unless, except
nōlo, nōlle (15) I am unwilling, I refuse
nōmen, nōminis, *n.* (11) name
    nōmine (11) by name, called
nōn (1) not
nōs we (acc. **nōs**, dat. **nōbīs**)
nōtus, -a, -um (11) known
novus, -a, -um (9) new
nox, noctis, *f.* (9) night
nūgae, nūgārum, *f. pl.* trifles, nonsense
nūllus, -a, -um (13) no
numquam (13) never
nunc (12) now
nūndinae, -ārum, *f. pl.* market day
nūntius, -ī, *m.* (12) messenger; message

obses, obsidis, *c.* (16) hostage
obsideō, obsidēre I besiege
occīdō, occīdere (7) I kill
occurrō, occurrere + dat. (11) I run to meet, I meet
oculus, -ī, *m.* (12) eye
olīva, -ae, *f.* olive; olive tree
omnis, omne (7) all
oppugnō, oppugnāre (7) I attack
ōrō, ōrāre (10) I beg, pray
ostendō, ostendere (11) I show

parātus, -a, -um (1) prepared, ready
parēns, parentis, *c.* (14) parent
parō, parāre (2) I prepare
parvus, -a, -um (9) small
pater, patris, *m.* (7) father
    patrēs, patrum, *m. pl.* senators
patria, -ae, *f.* (11) fatherland
paucī, -ae, -a (9) few
pauper, pauperis (15) poor
pāx, pācis, *f.* (16) peace
per + acc. (5) through, throughout
perficiō, perficere (12) I carry out, complete
perīculum, -ī, *n.* (10) danger
persuādeō, persuādēre + dat. I persuade
petō, petere (12) I seek, pursue, make for
pictūra, -ae, *f.* picture
placeō, placēre + dat. (12) I please
    mihi placet (12) it pleases me to, I decide
plērīque, plēraeque, pleraque several
pōnō, pōnere (5) I place
populus, -ī, *m.* (14) people
porta, -ae, *f.* (8) gate
portō, portāre (2) I carry
poscō, poscere (16) I demand
possum, posse (8) I am able to, I can
post + acc. (12) after
posteā (14) afterwards

postrīdiē (15) the next day
praebeō, praebēre I show
praesidium, -ī, *n.* (16) garrison
prīmum (adv.) (10) first
prīmus, -a, -um (6) first
prīnceps, prīncipis, *m.* (7) prince
prōcēdō, prōcēdere (4) I go forward, proceed
procul (15) far
proelium, -ī, *n.* (15) battle
prōferō, prōferre I carry forward, bring out
prōiciō, prōicere I throw forward, throw out
prope + acc. (6) near
Psȳchē, acc. **Psȳchēn**, *f.* Psyche
puella, -ae, *f.* (1) girl
puer, puerī, *c.* (3) boy; child
puerīlis, puerīle childish
pugna, -ae, *f.* (7) fight
pugnō, pugnāre (7) I fight
pulcher, pulchra, pulchrum (13) pretty, beautiful
pulsō, pulsāre I beat, knock

quaerō, quaerere (10) I ask; I look for
quantus, -a, -um? how big?
-que (8) and
quī, quae, quod (13) who, which
quīdam, quaedam, quoddam (14) a certain, a
quiēscō, quiēscere (10) I rest
quis? quid? (5) who? what?
quod (4) because
quōmodo? (15) how?
quoque (16) also

rapio, rapere I snatch
reddō, reddere (8) I give back, return
redeō, redīre (3) I go back, return
rēgia, -ae, *f.* palace
rēgīna, -ae, *f.* (11) queen
relinquō, relinquere (8) I leave behind
rēmigō, rēmigāre I row
repellō, repellere (15) I drive back
resistō, resistere + dat. (7) I resist
respondeō, respondēre (5) I answer
rēx, rēgis, *m.* (7) king
rogō, rogāre (5) I ask; I ask for
rumpō, rumpere (16) I break
rūsticus, -a, -um rustic, of the country

sacer, sacra, sacrum sacred
saepe (4) often
salutō, salutāre (2) I greet
salvē, salvēte! greetings!
saxum, -ī, *n.* (10) rock
scrībō, scrībere (6) I write
sed (1) but
sedeō, sedēre (3) I sit
semper (11) always
senātus, senātūs, *m.* (15) senate

senex, senis, *m.* (14) old man
sērō late
servō, servāre (8) I save
sī (13) if
sīc (9) thus, like that
silva, -ae, *f.* (10) wood
sōlus, -a, -um (8) alone
    nōn sōlum ... sed etiam (16) not only ... but also
somnus, -ī, *m.* (11) sleep
sonus, -ī, *m.* (13) sound
sordidus, -a, -um dirty
spectō, spectāre (5) I look at
squālidus, -a, -um filthy
statim (5) at once
statua, -ae, *f.* (16) statue
stō, stāre (11) I stand
stultus, -a, -um foolish
sub + abl. (10) under, at the foot of
subitō (2) suddenly
succurrō, succurrere + dat. (11) I run to help, I help
sum, esse I am
summus, -a, -um (16) highest, greatest
superō, superāre I overcome
supplicō, supplicāre + dat. I beseech, beg
surgō, surgere (4) I get up, rise
suus, -a, -um (14) his, her, their (own)

taberna, -ae, *f.* stall, shop, pub
tabula, -ae, *f.* writing tablet
taceō, tacēre (9) I am silent
tacitus, -a, -um (9) silent
tandem (4) at last
tantus, -a, -um (12) so great
tē (6) (acc. sing.) you
tempestās, tempestātis, *f.* storm
templum, -ī, *n.* (11) temple
temptō, temptāre (15) I try
teneō, tenēre (13) I hold
tergum, -ī, *n.* back
terra, -ae, *f.* (3) earth, land
terreō, terrēre I terrify
territus, -a, -um (8) terrified
tibi to you (sing.)
timeō, timēre (8) I fear, I am afraid
timidus, -a, -um fearful, timid
toga, -ae, *f.* (15) toga
togātus, -a, -um wearing a toga

tollō, tollere (10) I raise, lift
tōtus, -a, -um (9) whole
trādō, trādere (5) I hand over
trahō, trahere I drag
trāns + acc. (15) across
trēs, tria (5) three
trīstis, trīste (12) sad
Trōiānī, *m. pl.* Trojans
tū (6) you (sing.)
tum then
tuus, -a, -um (6) your

ubi (conjunction) (4) when
ubi? where?
Ulixēs, Ulixis, *m.* Ulysses = Odysseus
umquam (13) ever
unda, -ae, *f.* (10) wave
ūnus, -a, -um (5) one
urbs, urbis, *f.* (7) city
urna, -ae, *f.* water pot, urn
uxor, uxōris, *f.* (9) wife

valdē very
vehō, vehere I carry
vendō, vendere I sell
veniō, venīre (4) I come
ventus, -ī, *m.* (11) wind
Venus, Veneris, *f.* Venus
verbum, -ī, *n.* (10) word
vertō, vertere (8) I turn
via, -ae, *f.* (2) road, way
videō, vidēre (3) I see
vincō, vincere (7) I conquer
vīnum, -ī, *n.* (11) wine
vir, virī, *m.* (9) man
virgō, virginis, *f.* (16) maiden, virgin
virtūs, virtūtis, *f.* (16) courage, virtue
vīsō, vīsere I visit
vītō, vītāre I avoid
vīvō, vīvere (13) I live
vix (10) scarcely
vocō, vocāre (2) I call
volō, volāre I fly
volō, velle (15) I wish, I am willing
vōs (nom. & acc. plural) you
vōx, vōcis, *f.* (13) voice

Vocabulary

about **dē** + abl.
Aeneas **Aenēās, Aenēae,** *m.*
after **post** + acc.
again **iterum**
all **omnis, omne**
alone **sōlus, -a, -um**
already **iam**
always **semper**
am, I **sum, esse**
and **et**
and so **itaque**
anger **īra, īrae,** *f.*
angry **īrātus, -a, -um**
another **alius, alia, aliud**
anxious **ānxius, -a, -um**
approach, I **accēdō, accēdere**
arrive, I **adveniō, advenīre**
at last **tandem**

badly **male**
because **quod**
board, I **cōnscendō, cōnscendere**
boy **puer, puerī,** *m.*
bring, I **ferō, ferre**
build, I **aedificō, aedificāre**
but **sed**

call, I **vocō, vocāre**
can, I **possum, posse**
carry, I **portō, portāre**
children **puerī, puerōrum,** *m.*
city **urbs, urbis,** *f.*
climb, I **ascendō, ascendere**
come, I **veniō, venīre**
come back, I **redeō, redīre**
come in, I **intrō, intrāre**
comrade **comes, comitis,** *c.*
Cyclops **Cyclōps, Cyclōpis**

danger **perīculum, perīculī,** *n.*
daughter **fīlia, fīliae,** *f.*
decide, I **cōnstituō, cōnstituere**
Dido **Dīdō, Dīdōnis,** *f.*
dinner **cēna, cēnae,** *f.*
do, I **faciō, facere**
dog **canis, canis,** *c.*
don't **nōlī, nōlīte**
door **iānua, iānuae,** *f.*

enter, I **intrō, intrāre**

fame **fāma, fāmae,** *f.*

farmer **colōnus, colōnī,** *m.*
father **pater, patris,** *m.*
fear, I **timeō, timēre**
field **ager, agrī,** *m.*
finished **cōnfectus, -a, -um**
food **cibus, cibī,** *m.*
for **nam**
fountain **fōns, fontis** *m.*
friend **amīcus, amīcī,** *m.*
from **ā/ab** + abl.

gate **porta, portae,** *f.*
get up, I **surgō, surgere**
girl **puella, puellae,** *f.*
give, I **dō, dare**
glad **laetus, -a, -um**
go, I **eō, īre**
great **magnus, -a, -um**
Greeks **Graecī, Graecōrum,** *m. pl.*

hand over, I **trādō, trādere**
happy **laetus, -a, -um**
hard = diligently **dīligenter**
hear, I **audiō, audīre**
Hector **Hector, Hectōris,** *m.*
help, I **iuvō, iuvāre**
here **hīc;** to here **hūc**
here, I am **adsum, adesse**
hill **collis, collis,** *m.*
himself, herself, itself **ipse, ipsa, ipsum**
home (= to home) **domum**
horse **equus, equī,** *m.*
house **casa, casae,** *f.*
huge **ingēns, ingentis**
hurl, I **coniciō, conicere**
hurry, I **festīnō, festīnāre**

if **sī**
in **in** + abl.
into **in** + acc.

king **rēx, rēgis,** *m.*
known **nōtus, -a, -um**

land **terra, terrae,** *f.*
late **sērō**
lead, I **dūcō, dūcere**
learn, I **discō, discere**
leave, I **relinquō, relinquere**
letter **littera, litterae,** *f.*
listen to, I **audiō, audīre**
look! **ecce!**

look at, I **spectō, spectāre**

man **vir, virī**, *m.*
many **multī, multae, multa**
master (of school) **magister, magistrī**, *m.*
me **mē** (acc.), **mihi** (dat.)
meet, I **occurrō, occurrere** + dat.
mother **māter, mātris**, *f.*
mount (mountain) **mōns, montis**, *m.*
must, I **dēbeō, dēbēre**

near **prope** + acc.
no one **nēmō, nēminis**
not **nōn**
now **nunc**

often **saepe**
on **in** + abl.
order, I **iubeō, iubēre**
other **alius, alia, aliud**
    the other (= the rest) **cēterī, cēterae, cētera**
ought, I **dēbeō, dēbēre**

play, I **lūdō, lūdere**
please, I **placeō, placēre** + dat.
praise, I **laudō, laudāre**
prepare, I **parō, parāre**
prince **prīnceps, prīncipis**, *m.*

queen **rēgīna, rēgīnae**, *f.*
quickly **celeriter**

ready **parātus, -a, -um**
road **via, viae**, *f.*
receive, I **accipiō, accipere**
refuse, I **nōlō, nōlle**
rest, I **quiēscō, quiēscere**
return, I **redeō, redīre**
return (= give back), I **reddō, reddere**
road **via, viae**, *f.*
rock **saxum, saxī**, *n.*
Roman **Rōmānus, -a, -um**
run, I **currō, currere**
run up to, I **accurrō, accurrere**

sad **trīstis, trīste**
safe **incolumis, incolume**
sail, I **nāvigō, nāvigāre**
say, I **dīcō, dīcere**
says, he **inquit**
school **lūdus, lūdī**, *m.*
sea **mare, maris**, *n.*
see, I **videō, vidēre**
self (himself, herself, itself) **ipse, ipsa, ipsum**
send, I **mittō, mittere**
send back, I **remittō, remittere**
ship **nāvis, nāvis**, *f.*

shore **lītus, lītoris**, *n.*
shout, I **clāmō, clāmāre**
show, I **ostendō, ostendere**
silent **tacitus, -a, -um**
sit, I **sedeō, sedēre**
sky **caelum, caelī**, *n.*
sleep, I **dormiō, dormīre**
slowly **lentē**
soldier **mīles, mīlitis**, *m.*
son **fīlius, fīliī**, *m.*
soon **mox**
sound **sonus, sonī**, *m.*
stand, I **stō, stāre**
stay, I **maneō, manēre**
story **fābula, fābulae**, *f.*
suddenly **subitō**
suffering **labor, labōris**, *m.*
supper **cēna, cēnae**, *f.*

tablet (writing tablet) **tabula, tabulae**, *f.*
tell, I (a story) **nārrō, nārrāre**
tell (= say) **dīcō, dīcere**
temple **templum, templī**, *n.*
that **ille, illa, illud**
then (= next) **deinde**
there, I am **adsum, adesse**
this **hic, haec, hoc**
tired **fessus, -a, -um**
to **ad** + acc.
Trojans **Trōiānī, Trōiānōrum**, *m. pl.*

unwilling, I am **nōlō, nōlle**
us **nōs**; acc. **nōs**; dat. **nōbīs**

wait, I **maneō, manēre**
wait for, I **exspectō, exspectāre**
wake up, I **ēvigilō, ēvigilāre**
walk, I **ambulō, ambulāre**
want, I **cupiō, cupere**
war **bellum, bellī**, *n.*
water **aqua, aquae**, *f.*
well **bene**
what? **quid?**
when **ubi**
when? **quandō?**
while **dum**
who? **quis?**
why? **cūr?**
willing, I am **volō, velle**
wish, I **cupiō, cupere**; **volō, velle**
with **cum** + abl.
woman **fēmina, fēminae**, *f.*
word **verbum, -ī**, *n.*
work, I **labōrō, labōrāre**
write, I **scrībō, scrībere**

you *sing.* **tū, tē**; *pl.* **vōs, vōs**

Index of grammar

The numbers refer to chapters

Word-building